Working It Out

A Lesbian Relationship Primer

Frances Fuchs, PhD

BookSurge Publishing

Cover and interior design by Moira Hill with Frances Fuchs.
Illustrations by Sharon Neal Williams (scratch@sharonnealwilliams.com)

BOOKSURGE Publishing
7290-B Investment Drive, Charleston, South Carolina 29418
Telephone: 1-866-308-6235 Web Site: www.booksurge.com

ISBN 1-4392-5696-9

I dedicate this book to Gayle Remick and Den De Muri.
Gayle for teaching me about darts, devotion, loyalty, generosity of spirit
and loss. Den for teaching me about rivers, patience, serenity in
quietude, depth of feeling and the grace of acceptance. Each one in
their own way faced prejudice and hardship, challenged me and
consoled me, stood behind me and beside me through many ups and
downs. You have my abiding gratitude.

In Appreciation

This book would not have come about without the outpouring of stories from the many clients who honored me with their trust, sought guidance and shared their deepest needs, fears and hopes. You inspire and encourage me with your lives. Thank you for all of your feedback, input, enthusiasm and supportive inquiries about this project.

To my many friends and the queer community at large, you have been both familial balm and familial pain. I thank you for your solace, your diversity, your ideology and your willingness to "look again" at assumptions and priorities. I also wish to thank my "readers," those women who read the manuscript and gave me valuable feedback and essential editing (Subie your attention to detail was remarkably helpful).

Great appreciation goes to my editor, Suzanne Sherman for clearing up the verbal clutter and clarifying the ideas; and to the illustrator Sharon Neal Williams for her creativity and talent.

Through many resurrections of this book over the years there are a number of people who's belief and support have sustained me personally and professionally. I want to thank Peter Krohn and Dinah Bachrach of the Couples Center in Sebastopol, California for the ongoing dialogue about couples counseling theory and practice and for their personal sharing, vulnerability, encouragement and care. Many thanks as well for the strength of friends and colleagues, Roberta Goldfarb and Barbara Vass Harwood.

I owe much to my parents, Lawrence Fuchs and Natalie Rogers, who instilled in me a sense of purpose and possibility, compassion and kindness. Both talented and accomplished writers and teachers, they nurtured my abilities, taught me to question, to think and to act.

And most importantly, I wish to acknowledge my dear longtime friend and colleague Mary Hinsdale for launching this project with me (originally as co-authors). Through many hours of collaboration, discussion, working and writing together she maintained her authenticity and dedication, and her delightfully wicked sense of humor. She is one of the clearest, smartest and kindest women I know, and while her life and ideas took her in a different direction from this book, our friendship and deep regard continue on a single path. Without her this book would not exist.

> Frances Fuchs
> September 8, 2009
> Santa Rosa, California

Contents

List of Exercises

We are shaped by our perceptions,
by the story we tell ourselves over and over about real
or imagined slights and injustices in our lives.

We collect incidents that support our story.
Our minds seek to make sense of our feelings and we create that story
from imperfect perceptions and projections, that are only
a part of the whole picture.

Remember, your relationship is much more than
the story you tell yourself about it.

You can be relieved of the pain of resentment and wounding
by opening your vision wider to include compassion
for your own and others human frailties and limitations.

If you look at your partner through a wider lens
of experience and empathy you may see her value and strengths
in balance with her limitations.

From this place you can make clear choices,
including the choice to change yourself.

If you feel stuck,
be open to a slight shift in perspective,
an opening of the lens of perception,
or a change in the story line.

ᐧᐧ Introduction ᐧᐧ

"I hear the singing of the lives of women,
The clear mystery, the offering and pride."
MURIEL RUKEYSER

In 1991 Mary Hinsdale and I led the first groups for lesbian couples in our area, Sonoma County, California. It was wonderful to have a room full of lesbian couples sharing intimate issues, problems and solutions with each other. Their emotional growth and successes in building relationship skills was inspiring.

In preparation for the groups, we searched for published materials for lesbian couples. Finding few at all and none that fit our needs, we developed our own exercises and informational handouts for our groups and clients. We also wanted an educational and practical tool that individuals and couples could use on their own. Thus, the idea for this book was born.

We thought it would be easy; we thought it would be fun. On many occasions this has been true. What we predominantly found, however, was that with full-time counseling practices and life's significant twists and turns this book took twelve years to complete. Along the way, Mary became a mom and she was no longer had "extra time" to devote to this project. I continued on, with her blessing, stealing time from my practice, a week here and a week there.

During the eighteen years since those first groups I have both weathered the depths of relationship despair and loss as well as the heights of relationship delight and commitment. Experiences that contained profound endings and beginnings woven together with predicaments and dilemmas familiar to many lesbians in our time: numerous foiled yet meaningful attempts at obtaining legal status as a married lesbian couple; sixteen years of committed relationship ending in widowhood thus becoming single in midlife; dating in the time of AIDS; a bisexual lifestyle change — partnering with a man and facing identity shock and criticism, then finding my footing again.

It remains my conviction, affirmed by professional and personal experience, that the quest for satisfying and loving relationships is a human need and a worthwhile goal, and it is attainable. This book is based on that conviction.

I want couples and individuals to know that relationships are not just confusing, messy and chaotic. Even in the worst of times (and in the best) there can be some sense to what is going on. Others have explored this territory before, and everyone can take hope, information and courage from their experience.

A significant difference between heterosexual and lesbian relationships are the effects of homophobia. Another notable difference stems from the divergent gender socialization that women and men receive. The physiological differences between men and women in brain function, hormones and their effects on relational preferences and behaviors are another factor. This combination of socialization and physiology accounts for the sex roles we learn, reject, remodel and live out. And since sex role expectations, ethnocultural backgrounds and economic distinctions account for much of the difference between men and women in our culture, therein lie most differences between gay male and lesbian subcultures.

While the divergent cultural experiences of men and women result in contrasts among heterosexual and lesbian and gay male relationships, I believe that the emotional and verbal skills necessary to build and maintain healthy relationships are universal. However, I've approached learning and applying these skills from a perspective I believe is most suited to lesbian relationships. This approach has a female viewpoint, and the examples are drawn from lesbian individuals and couples. The author holds a feminist perspective, recognizing the effects of biological, economic and social differences for men and women. While the Euro-American perspective values the individual rights over the collective good, there are many cultures that hold the needs of community and/or family over individual concerns. I hold that both are necessary and interdependent. The balance of individual, relationship, family and community rights and needs is a foundation of health. I hope that readers examine the influences of these issues on their lives and relationships.

Chapter 1, "Ways To Use This Book" supplies information on the applications of this book, as well as guidelines and suggestions for starting groups and use with a professional counselor.

Chapters 2 through 5 give an overview of early relationship stages and important personal skills needed to make relationships work. Chapter 6 addresses coming out and being out, an important and ever-present issue influencing our lives and relationships.

Chapter 7 reviews the cycles of long-term coupling. This vantage point enables you to locate yourselves much like a "You Are Here" map. Information is provided on how to successfully traverse and persevere through the conflicted storms, desolate deserts and tight passages that all couples face at some time.

Chapters 8 and 9 focus on specific emotional and verbal skills needed for success during all portions of your journey. Communication is that complex interplay between words, tone of voice, body language, timing and intent. Communication includes knowing when to be quiet, how to listen with compassion and understanding, and how to get your point across. Exercises on popular topics such as how to have a productive conversation about emotionally charged matters without getting entangled and how to fight fair, are provided to assist in honing those skills.

A single women's symbol (♀) is used to designate an exercise to be done individually and a double women's symbol (⚢) to designate an exercise to be done as a couple.

I use the terms "partner" and "lover" to mean a woman with whom you are emotionally and romantically involved. The term "friend" is used to denote a person with whom you are emotionally involved but not romantically involved. While the language in much of this book is geared toward couples that are romantically involved, the principles and skills developed are relevant to any friendship that involves emotional intimacy. I have attempted to use language that is inclusive of this when possible.

You will notice that throughout this book there are reminders to "pause and reflect." Introspection, understanding and retention all play a part in developing the awareness and the life skills needed to have successful relationships. The process of pausing and reflecting on what has been written has been shown to increase one's ability to remember and integrate the information in daily life. For those of you who don't like to write, use the method of pause and reflect in the exercises to get the most out of them.

Pause & Reflect

Working It Out is intended to be useful to both individuals and couples. It is easy to imagine we know the "right" ways to have successful relationships when sitting in an armchair reading about them. It is much more difficult to actually apply what we know to our own tangled and complex web of interactions. If you simply read this book you will learn something. If you actually do the exercises, have discussions with your partners and friends, and pay attention to your self, you will change something.

I hope at all times to remind you of the humor and humanness of life. I hope that you remain true to yourself, and allied with the significant others you relate to. Honesty and heart go a long way in reaching the destination of loving, fulfilling relationships. If that is what you desire, it is that destination I wish for you.

— FRANCES FUCHS, PhD

Ways To Use This Book

Whatever drew you to pick up this book will determine how you use it. Sometimes an individual's preferred mode for using this book is very similar to her partner's (lucky you!). When it isn't (which often happens) it's time to experiment and see what fits. Each partner must honor her own and her partner's limits and pace. Breaks are as necessary as engaged focus.

One can get overly invested in using this workbook the "right way" or resist using it at all. Both of these wreak havoc and slow progress. Try one method; if it doesn't work, try something a little different. Remember, the experience and the outcome, not the form, are the priorities.

By Yourself

One way to use this book is to read it by yourself. Whether you're in a coupled relationship or not, this information may give you newfound understanding about your interactions with others. Doing the exercises independently will give you further insight into your dynamics. The exercises to be done on your own are marked with this symbol: ♀.

With Your Partner

Using this book as a team, your individual and collective concerns as a couple will direct your focus. The exercises to be done together are marked with this symbol: ⚤, and will generate a good deal of discussion. Or a couple can work parallel (setting aside time to read and do the exercises in the same room, each with your own workbook, with a minimum of interaction). Your personalities and individual modes of operation will determine what works best. The mutual respect and acceptance you extend each other are the biggest determinants of a good experience and a productive outcome.

The energy and time you invest in this book is a valuable contribution to improving your relationship skills. There are no wasted efforts! Just remember to use the safety guidelines described here. These may include the use of active listening, time-outs, taking turns, establishing beginning and ending times, and selecting a neutral place free from intrusion in which to work. The goal is to facilitate each participant feeling safe enough to express herself and risk being vulnerable, to support each person's best self and contain one's reactive defenses. To do this effectively, it is necessary to have mutual agreement, consistency, follow-up on plans and commitments, and sometimes, to renegotiate needed changes.

Start Your Own Peer Group

One exciting and productive way to work on relationship issues is in a group of other lesbians. It could be a group designated for couples or a mixed group of couples and singles desiring to work on their relationships. A group is a wonderful way to share ideas and find out that your problems are not so terrible or unique. Although you can feel less vulnerable when you keep your problems and struggles to yourselves, there is tremendous healing in breaking through the isolation many lesbian couples face. In the many groups we have facilitated, new friends were made and new insights gained. Women renewed their love and partnerships while improving their understanding of what it takes to "make it work."

In a leaderless peer group we recommend that the emphasis be on education rather than group therapy. Refrain from criticizing, advice-giving, and trying to "fix" someone's problems. Speak simply from your own experience. If suggestions are solicited, proceed tenderly. See Appendix A for a more complete set of suggestions and guidelines.

Starting a Professionally Facilitated Couples Group

This workbook can be used as a guide for professionals facilitating lesbian couples groups. The groups that we lead are a combination of educational presentation, discussion, personal sharing and support, and skill-building exercises. A counselor familiar with lesbian and couples' issues can also be expected to add her own information and case examples to the presentations. And having a competent facilitator adds a level of emotional safety with the professional experience.

If there are not groups like this in your area, you can start one by finding a therapist with experience facilitating groups and proposing a group such as the one described above for peer groups. Often, therapists are more than willing to lead groups if you can organize a minimum number of couples who are committed to meeting and offer a location for it.

The format and guidelines offered for peer groups will also be appropriate to a professionally-led group, adjusting the format to add more time for group process, couples-counseling demonstrations, and role playing. The fee structure can be jointly determined by the therapist(s) and organizer(s). Information about the fees should be added to the guidelines, and the section on absences should be amended. (See Appendix A.)

Initiating Use with Your Couples Counselor

If using this book on your own does not bring desired results, consider using a counselor's help. Working with an objective and professionally trained third party can make a world of difference. If you are seeing a couples counselor now to help with difficult issues in your relationship, you can introduce the exercises in this book as a complement to your counseling. Sometimes a couple is overwhelmed and confused when confronting problems. Reviewing the information in these chapters can assist you in clarifying an area or areas of focus in a more systematic way. Sessions with your counselor may be put to more specific use, saving you time and money.

Use By Counselors in Couples' Sessions

As a professional counselor, you may sometimes wish for specific tools to use with your clients in couples. Using this book as an educational device will speed your clients' progress in their sessions. By assigning pertinent chapters and exercises as "homework" you will generate a focus on specific problem areas and teach healthy communication patterns. Many of the exercises are appropriate for use in the counseling session, such as "Active Listening," in which coaching your clients as they practice is often a benefit. By familiarizing yourself with this material and using it in tandem with your own methods of counseling you'll find openings in previously blocked areas.

Chapter 2

Dating

"Never grow a wishbone, daughter, where your backbone ought to be."
CLEMENTINE PADDLEFORD

Ahh, dating. A word that brings terror to some, delight to others and a bit of both to most of us. There is the thrill and sense of exploration, but given the clammy hands, dry mouth, and awkwardness of it all — can dating be fun? It depends on past experiences, openness to adventure, sense of self, and, of course, one's goals.

Once you're out of the dating scene for any length of time it can be difficult to get back in. It often feels like time travel. Poof! You're seventeen again. Adolescent awkwardness and hormones come rushing back. A calm, mature attorney in the afternoon is a bumbling idiot by evening. A competent, thoughtful carpenter by day is a nervous ninny at night.

Those on the cutting edge of dating seem to be the extroverts. They are assertive by nature, bold by birth. It is harder for the introverts, the shy ones who would rather eat worms than pick up the phone to call that cute stranger they met at the laundromat.

Here is a brief guide to dating for your enjoyment and edification. May it stimulate much thought and discussion. Keep your eyes open and your feet on the ground.

Why Date?

Dating serves three functions: companionship, search for a long-term partner, and the beginning stage of an ongoing relationship. It is helpful to know what your intentions are (for yourself as much as for others). Knowing your intentions eliminates troublesome, indirect ways of meeting your needs.

Sometimes dating is used to prove something. For example, it can be used to prove to your ex-lovers that you, too, are a hot item or to prove to yourself that you're desirable and sophisticated. A dating frenzy (unceasing flirtations, over-booked social calendar, dog hasn't been walked in weeks and no time for yourself) can be used to avoid uncomfortable feelings or life circumstances.

There are many definitions of what constitutes dating activity, and rightly so. You and your companion need not necessarily know whether a particular activity is a date or not. At some point, however, it's necessary to put your cards on the table for the sake of clarity and ethics. Knowing each other's intentions allows each participant to shape her expectations accordingly and make her own choices.

Dating is an opportunity to get to know women you're interested in and check out what kind of relationship may develop. It isn't always obvious if the initial attraction to someone will be romantic, platonic or some combination of the two. Dating may or may not include sexual intimacy. Dating can simply be a less pressured means of enjoying someone's company.

Even with conscious goals, it must be noted that these are dynamic matters of the heart, libido and unknown recesses of the subconscious. Many a roving eye determined to enjoy various flowers in the garden has found a particular bloom so interesting and compelling, so fragrant and lush, that she found herself lingering. Settling down urges come from within and lo — she's planted. Curiously, those seemingly determined to find that "special one" have sometimes found satisfaction enjoying a bouquet of experiences.

If you're clear that a long-term partnership is your desire, your intentions can be made known early on and your activities will be geared towards finding out as much as possible about this person. Remember, though, this process is ideally fun and companionable — not a headhunt. Getting to know someone is a necessary first stage of any long-term relationship — whether it turns out to be a friendship, an acquaintance or lover.

Is She or Isn't She?

One of our first tasks — finding out if she's a dyke — can be quite nerve-wracking given the inherent dangers of living, working and socializing in a homophobic culture. To determine her interest and availability, powers of observation and

"Gaydar"

6

creative investigation are sometimes needed. As members of an invisible and discriminated against minority our means of identifying each other as "club members" range from the subtle to the overt. Plumage, costumes, verbal cues, interests, friends, and, yes, lapel buttons are all used to help us recognize each other. Questions you ask yourself during this stage might be: "Did she mention any lesbian performers? Does she have any queer friends? She has a great leather jacket, she repairs her own Honda and she likes Ellen Degeneres…" Of course, if no clues appear you can take a bold step and ask her.

How do you identify yourself as a lesbian to her? In order to make connections with other lesbians you must let yourself be known. Anyone for a few rounds of "Oooooohhh, I enjoy being a dyke…"?

To communicate interest, flirtation is often employed. Flirtation, an art in itself, can be simply enjoying a current attraction or it can be a way to let her know you want more. An extra-bright smile, catching her eye for an extended glance, or a squeeze of her hand are favorites. There is, however, such a thing as compulsive flirting. This is flirting regardless of the negative effects it might have on you or others, flirting as a way to manipulate, or flirting when it's clearly inappropriate. If those around you seem uncomfortable, best to check in with yourself and get clear on your behavior and motives.

If you have a compelling interest in someone it is strongly recommended, even advised, that you check out the terrain before running head-long into romantic pursuit. Platonic activities such as having coffee, going to the movies, or taking walks or hikes, allow both of you to find out more with some objectivity, wisdom and grace. Ask yourself "Is this someone I can be friends with?" If an honest answer is accompanied with a green light, it is time to employ more overt dating efforts.

Etiquette

Each culture and subculture has its own code of etiquette. Even the lesbian community has its Ms. Manners.

Etiquette was originally designed to avoid conflict — to prevent skirmishes and wars. Once learned and agreed upon, these codes allowed potential enemies and fellow clan members to know what to expect from others and what was expected from them in social interactions. Like shaking hands, it was a means of communicating good will; of showing that one was among friends not foes.

In its best application, etiquette is used to enable all participants to feel comfortable, safe and well regarded. Pragmatically, it makes certain tasks easier, for example, feeding ourselves and enjoying conversation with others in the same setting. In this case, the code says, "Don't talk with your mouth full." The crucial factor is that the participants know and use the same code.

In this light, etiquette offers a common standard and consistent set of rituals that can be comforting as we attempt to inhabit close spaces with one another.

Individual values and experience determine our dating etiquette. We come to the awareness of our grand state of lesbianism with a plethora of etiquettes. Our families of origin, class, ethnic and regional cultures, religions, the generation into which we were born, and our experiences, shape our internal codes of behavior and values. Instead of a lack of "how-to's" and "what-to-do's" we are awash in directives. Do any of them fit our lesbian lifestyle?

Ideally, dating etiquette enables us to use our own communication style and respect all parties as we go through this selection process. Etiquette helps participants be more comfortable in this vulnerable "exploration stage." Though she is an outlaw to society, even the most daring "lesberado" occasionally yearns for safe cover or a little guidance.

Initiating

Knowing whether an invitation is actually a date or not is often a mystery. In our culture women are not well taught to initiate a romantic relationship. Both women can be waiting for the other to indicate romantic or platonic intent, rather than risk vulnerability. Defining a shared activity as romantic can be as simple as bringing her a flower, sending her a card, or by saying, "Would you like to go on a REAL date with me?" Regardless of creativity or subtlety, these actions always require vulnerability. Rejection is a possibility. Kindness to oneself and the other is the key to retaining self-esteem regardless of the outcome.

Who Pays?

"Who pays for what" is fraught with meanings…implied obligations (you owe me), gender identity (butch/femme), superior financial status (provider). If you wish to treat your date to entertainment or dinner, it is best to inquire if that's OK. A refusal of your generosity need not mean disinterest, but it may reflect issues of parity, autonomy and who knows what else. Explore a little further to see if she may have a suggestion or another preference.

8

EXERCISE 1 — Dating Grace   ♀

The following questions are designed to help you become familiar with your dating values, needs and intentions.

1. Describe an interaction you observed or had with someone (if not in a dating scenario, then a social setting) where one person was particularly gracious and enabled you to feel regarded and comfortable.

2. Describe a situation in which you demonstrated graciousness that enabled another to feel regarded and comfortable. What were your best characteristics in this situation?

3. Describe one of the best acts of initiating you have observed between women. How did it make you feel?

4. Describe the worst initiating actions or gestures that you've made or received. How did you feel?

Grace, Faith and Prudence, Out for a Walk

9

Ethical Dating

Ethics are a conscious set of principles, beliefs and values that determine conduct. Whether we know it or not, our values determine much of our behavior. Honesty, integrity, consideration and reliability are positive dating values. Actions based on these values communicate respect, enhance self-esteem and bring out the best in anyone. With these values in mind, you can prevent messy emotional residue requiring major cleanup later. The following section will help you come to know and clarify your values. Ethical dating is worth the effort.

EXERCISE 2 — Dating Faith   ♀

1. List the dating ethics that are important to you:

2. How many of these do you demonstrate on a regular basis?

3. If a friend were to describe your ethics, what would they say?

Clarity and Intentions

Kind honesty and tactful directness are crucial to good communication. To be honest we must know our own feelings, assumptions and intentions, and then we must take a risk and let them be known to our date. This means speaking them out loud, not just hinting. Similarly, one must also believe what one is being told by her (unless you have intuition or evidence to the contrary). For example, it is not fair, or promising, to date someone who says she does not want a long-term relationship when you do (or vise versa).

EXERCISE 3 — Dating Prudence ♀

1. Take a moment to ask yourself what your intentions are in your
   current situation.

Pause & Reflect

2. What do you know or assume about hers? If you are not dating now, think back to your
   dating days.

3. What have you done to let her know your intentions?

Adultery

Adultery happens if a prior agreement between two parties for an exclusive sexual relationship
is broken. The person primarily responsible for breaking an agreement is the one who made it
(i.e. the woman in the monogamous relationship). However, if you
are in the position of wanting to date a "married" woman, you
should carefully consider your own ethical stance. How do
you feel about contributing to the breaking of an
agreement and, if the situation were reversed,
would you want your relationship to be
treated that way? A good rule of thumb is to
"Do unto others as you would have them do
unto you" not "Do others before they do
you."

Predatory Behavior

Have you ever watched a vulture hungrily circling above
a dying animal? They are waiting to feed and depend on

this food for their survival. Have you ever seen a fellow lesbian woo a woman whose relationship is in turmoil? They too are exhibiting predatory behavior. This human predatory behavior is usually based on an assumption of scarcity and a fear of being alone. We do not need to be in a relationship to survive, but it can sometimes feel that way. There are plenty of great women out there who are available. No one needs to wait on the sidelines for a couple to break up and then pounce. Hovering over a relationship that is struggling to survive is not only unethical and unsavory; it gives us all a bad name. It brings drama and turmoil to each member involved. Instead, couples should be given support in dealing with the difficulties of healing a relationship and/or breaking up in a nondestructive manner. Advice such as, "Just leave her, she's no good" rarely helps. If, in the course of dating, you have found yourself growing wings and a long, hooked beak, don't despair. Take a long hard look, and cut it out.

Affection and Sex

Physically affectionate and sexual behaviors during dating can range from hand holding and sitting close to kissing, "petting," and "doing the wild thing." These can each be fun, exciting, comforting, and enjoyable, or uncomfortable, distasteful, or scary, depending on your individual experience. Kissing does not necessarily have to lead to more; each level of physical intimacy is yours to choose.

It is a common experience for women that sexual activity greatly increases emotional vulnerability, intimacy and investment in another person. If there is strong chemistry between women, the intense sexual energy can override the useful caution of the intellect and dictate the pace and course of the relationship. There is nothing quite so powerful to change expectations and implied commitment than becoming sexual early in a dating experience. The best this author can advise is to keep your wits about you and be scrupulously honest with yourself and your date(s).

Safe Sex

As lesbians we too often think ourselves immune to the AIDS virus. We hear that we are the group at lowest risk, and while it is true that woman to woman transmission of HIV is not statistically significant, all it takes for personal significance is to have it happen to you or a loved one.

This as an ethical issue. Your responsibility is as vital as your new lover's to reveal important information about exposure. To be ethical, practice these steps:

1. Search the very recesses of your memory to find all the sexual experiences you have had in the last ten years (yes, count 'em, ten). Talk with a new lover about your sexual pasts to determine the risk factors for HIV (and other Sexually Transmitted Diseases such as HPV, Hepatitis, or Herpes).

Safe Sex

A woman is at risk for HIV if in the last ten years she has had:

- ▾ intravenous drug use
- ▾ unprotected sex with a man or a woman at risk
- ▾ blood transfusions
- ▾ occupational exposure (needle punctures, contact with blood products)

2. Get tested for HIV. (County health facilities usually offer free, confidential testing with a simple swab of your gums. It takes only twenty minutes to get the results.) At the time of this writing it has been determined that one must have had no possible HIV exposure (sexual contact or other exposure factors listed above) in the last six months for a test to be fully accurate because the HIV virus can be present but undetectable in the first six months of infection. If you have had any exposure in the last six months then you must test now and again six months later for accuracy to be totally sure. Ask your new lover to get tested and wait for test results until you choose to have unprotected sexual contact. There is no issue of impropriety, being overly intimate, or untrusting when asking an intended sexual partner to be tested. If you are going to be sexual with her, knowledge of life-threatening exposure is your right.

3. Follow safe-sex practices as outlined below if there is any exposure to risk or if you just can't bring yourself to ask at this stage of relating.

4. If you choose to have a monogamous relationship, maintain safe sex practices for six months and then get tested. Only after six months and you've both tested negative is it safe to have unprotected sex.

Safe Sex Guidelines for Lesbians at Risk

These guidelines are intended for lesbians who have reason to believe they may be HIV positive or whose activities may place them at risk. If either woman may be carrying the virus, she should not allow her menstrual blood, vaginal secretions, urine, feces or breast milk to enter her partner's body through the mouth, rectum, vagina or through broken skin (this includes small cuts on the hands). Although the virus has been found in saliva, there is no evidence that it can be transmitted through that fluid.

Safe Sex Practices

Massage, hugging, social (dry) kissing, body-to-body rubbing, voyeurism, exhibitionism, fantasy, touching your own genitals (masturbation), vibrators or other sex toys (using your own only on yourself or using hers only on her or using a fresh condom over a shared toy), S/M or other activities that do not involve the exchange of body fluids.

Possibly Safe Sex Practices

Oral-genital contact (cunnilingus) using a thin piece of latex placed between the vulva and tongue, hand/finger-to-genital contact, vaginal or anal penetration with finger(s) using a disposable latex glove, external urine contact, anal-oral contact (rimming) with a latex barrier.

Unsafe Sex Practices

Unprotected oral-genital contact (cunnilingus), especially during menstruation; unprotected hand/finger-to-vagina or anus contact, especially if you have cuts on hands; sharing needles (IV needles, body piercing needles), blood contact of any kind, including menstrual blood; urine or feces in mouth or vagina; unprotected anal-oral contact (rimming); hand in rectum/vagina (fisting); sharing sex toys that have contact with body fluids.

If you have sex with men practice safe sex only, learn about condoms and always use them.

If You Are Exposed

If you find out that you have been exposed to the HIV virus there are currently drug combinations to take that can stop the virus at the onset, before it has a chance to fully establish itself in your system. This would be the case if you found out that your new sexual partner is HIV positive. With early intervention most other STD's can be successfully treated or slowed as well. Remember this motto: "No Blame, No Shame, Get Help."

EXERCISE 4 — Rate Your Sexual Risk   ♀

1. Make a written list of all the people you have been sexual with in the last ten years. After each person's name list the sexual activities you engaged in, from smooching to smoldering. Now check the list of activities against the list of "at risk" behaviors. Also think and write down what you know about the histories of these partners and their "at risk" activities. This exercise will give you a start at determining whether you are at risk due to sexual activity.

Pause & Reflect

2. What information do you wish that your past or present lover(s) had shared with you before you had sex?

3. What information about sex do you wish you had shared that you didn't?

Reckless Abandon, Lust and Fun

After identifying your values, clarifying your intentions, minding your manners and practicing safe sex you may be asking, "What about reckless abandon, lust and fun?" YES! YES! YES! Let's heartily applaud those. Believe it or not, dating is still an adventure. To these ends...

May you sashay boldly, explore gently,
and enjoy each other thoroughly with kindness,
honesty, and adventuresome spirit!

Chapter 3

Challenges To Lasting Primary Relationships

"Sooner or later we all discover that the important
moments in life are not the advertised ones, not the birthdays,
the graduations, the weddings, not the great goals achieved.
The real milestones are less prepossessing.
They come to the door of memory unannounced,
stray dogs that amble in, sniff around a bit, and never leave.
Our lives are measured by these."
SUSAN B. ANTHONY

One stereotype about lesbians is that we are incapable of lasting relationships. While heterosexual couples are pressured to remain together no matter what, the reverse is often true for lesbian couples. Instead of receiving advice to stick it out, many a lesbian with relationship trouble is advised to find somebody new. In spite of this, we can and do establish and maintain long-term, committed, healthy relationships. These relationships can be characterized by stability, mutual caring, generosity, love, and support. It is my experience that most women desire to be in lasting relationships with a sense of security, depth and history.

Another stereotype is that long-term sexual relationships are the only valid way to relate and that all others (e.g., friendship, serial monogamy, polyamory, dating, non-sexual partnerships, lesbian family) are always of lesser value and lower priority. This perspective and value system is carried over from heterosexual relationship criteria, and if this model doesn't fit it may result in shame and internal conflict. If we unconsciously internalize this value system we risk negating what may be our richest and most satisfying relationships.

Every human interaction gives us the opportunity to apply what we know and to learn what we don't know. A 36-year friendship offers different gifts and opportunities than a three-week affair. Neither is "better than" the other and each challenges us to grow in our ability to love and be loved. We can act on our true preferences only after our imaginations expand past the limitations of the models given to us.

Primary Relationship as a Path of Growth

This being said most of those reading this book are seeking to find, or improve a primary relationship, one that provides lasting companionship and mutual support. Ideally, these relationships enhance the quality of our lives. A common illusion is that we find someone who has characteristics or "pieces" we're missing; the object is to team up with them and claim those pieces by association. This form of relating contains the belief that people, places and things can fix us. We mistakenly believe they are the sources of wholeness and happiness, and that we therefore need them to be whole in ourselves. While it is a natural human need to bond with others, a fundamental task is to become more whole ourselves as we experience the joys and challenges of connecting intimately with another person. Developing what is incomplete within us happens while we enjoy and learn from the relationship. This learning includes acceptance of ourselves as we are, of the other person as she is, and maintaining a healthy connection despite our differences.

Challenges to Lesbian Relationships

Few Role Models/Lesbian Invisibility

None of us was raised to be lesbian. Until very recently one never saw positive lesbian relationships portrayed in the literature and entertainment media. Even now it is rare. When we are involved with another woman we cross previous boundaries, defy expectations, break taboos. Without new role models we flounder around or dive recklessly back into more traditional family patterns. Some of these patterns are fraught with sexism. The invisibility of lesbian relationships in the dominant culture is a covert message that we don't or shouldn't exist. But we also have a great opportunity. Divesting ourselves of previously oppressive models gives us freedom to create more egalitarian relationships. We have the option to take what we need and leave the rest.

Few Accepted Rituals

Societal and familial rituals (such as acknowledging weddings and anniversaries, gift-giving, births and deaths) give validity and respect to heterosexual couples who make public commitments. They are powerful forms reinforcing the mainstream heterosexual model of "family." Other types of acknowledgments for heterosexual couples include special vacation rates, club memberships, seating and sleeping arrangements at family gatherings, and visual validation through advertising, film and print media. These blend together to make the cultural "soup stock" that we swim in and consume daily. The lack of support of lesbian couples is demonstrated by the lack of similar rituals available to us. Acknowledging the manner of our relationships and lesbian "family networks" (committed friendship groups that serve many of the same functions as family members) requires effort, creativity and persistence. Those efforts pay rich and lasting dividends in feelings of validation, belonging, security and self-esteem.

Few Legal Benefits

Maintaining and respecting the integrity and privacy of family life is acknowledged legal precedent for heterosexually defined families. Property and parental rights settlements are outlined by law in the case of death or divorce. At this time lesbian and gay families are not acknowledged and/or are often considered to be unfit or inappropriate environments for natural, adopted, or foster children. Lesbian partners can not generally share employee health and retirement benefits. In cases of lesbian "divorce" there is little legal precedent for the rights of non-biological mothers. Unless specific arrangements are made by partners, property, estates and child custody do not automatically go to the surviving spouse. By making specific legal arrangements, we can assume responsibility for our own protection to the extent of the law. Even though there are many legal limitations and no absolute guarantees with these actions, they are acts of empowerment and affirmation to ourselves and our relationships. They are part of the many steps to equality.

Fewer Financial Benefits

Lesbian households often have lower combined income and fewer financial resources than heterosexual or gay male households due to the lesser earning power of women. It may be beneficial to pool resources with another, but we may derive little financial benefit from doing so with another woman. Tax structures are designed for heterosexual couples or single people — not lesbian and gay couples. In public service and corporate worlds a stable heterosexual marriage is considered an asset, at times a prerequisite, to career advancement and the income that comes with it, whereas a lesbian relationship is often a liability in the straight world.

Given such lack of financial benefits, it might be surmised that lesbian couplings would thereby be freed from such influences as marrying for money or dating for status. But alas, we are human and as influenced by such superficialities as anyone. Similar to any minority culture, we develop our own status symbols based on different values, (e.g., politically correct vs. politically incorrect, feminist vs. non-feminist, well-read vs. TV junkie, jock vs. couch potato). Some status symbols are in rebellion to or in compliance with the dominant culture (e.g. insistent downward mobility or obsessive upward mobility, valuing only long-term relationships or only brief involvements, dating only women from a particular class background). If unconscious these reactions keep us stuck in self-limiting patterns.

Lack of Support From the Lesbian Community

It's sad to say, but there is often a profound lack of support from the people whom we expect it from the most — our own community. Perhaps we mimic the culture at large, or perhaps our internalized homophobia has us believing the straight party line. Our own judgments and fears frequently lead to criticism and indirect carping. "Dump her," is said too fast, and too often. Contrary to popular belief jumping on the anger wagon and joining in a mudslinging fest is not the loving thing to do for a friend with relationship woes. We each need a neutral place to vent our hurt and angry feelings. Advice-giving and gossiping do not a good friend make. A compassionate and non-judgmental ear allows for clearing the air without toxic side effects.

Lack of Familial Support

I've already discussed the negative effects of heterosexually oriented family rituals that exclude us in symbol, intent and participation. Would your family members respond differently to your enthusiastic description of the new romantic interest in your life if "she" were a "he"? Regrettably, most of us would have to say yes. Herein is the double bind of homophobia: we must choose to risk rejection and disapproval in openly expressing our interests, attractions and joys, or hide and contain ourselves to maintain family relationships that are important to us. The first option gives the possibility of honest support or the potential of negative judgment and rejection. The second option insures that we will not receive familial support for our relationships. We may have more leeway than we think. Families have more potential for accepting or adjusting than they may initially show, though positive responses may take years. We cannot insist our families fall in love or even have close relations with our partner, but we can give them that opportunity. In this way we are active agents in bringing more wholeness to our lives.

Ideally, families are sources of physical and emotional support to their members. Even geographically scattered families share resources such as treasured hand-me-downs, consumer information and pertinent family history. These exchanges give us feelings of continuity, belonging, and pragmatic support. We "the givers and receivers" all suffer losses when we can not avail ourselves of this support. These homophobic blocks can result in our questioning whether or not it's worth it to be in a lesbian relationship. Finding and building supportive connections among our original and our chosen networks of family and friends is crucial to our well-being.

Homophobia

We often blame ourselves or each other for the pain and alienation caused by homophobia. So in the interest of liberating ourselves from the sticky goo of the homophobic tar pits, the following is a list of some of the negative effects this plague has on forming lasting, healthy relationships.

Homophobia:

▼ inhibits self-esteem (the basis for healthy relationships)

▼ isolates us from each other, making it difficult to find one another

- ▼ limits our sources of support and encouragement for dating, socializing and establishing relationships

- ▼ limits the places and events where we feel comfortable dating and socializing

- ▼ limits the financial, legal, societal and familial benefits of being in a relationship

- ▼ excludes our relationships from validating rituals and rites of passage

- ▼ excludes us from informal and supportive familial and societal networks

- ▼ makes lesbian relationships and lesbian families seem non-existent

- ▼ results in a lack of role models for lesbian relationships of all kinds

- ▼ isolates lesbian families from each other

- ▼ creates conflicts in our relationships about being or not being out

- ▼ raises questions about safety and inclusion in the larger society regarding our children

- ▼ threatens parental rights and child custody for lesbian parents

- ▼ prevents lesbians from providing foster care and easily adopting children

- ▼ prevents and limits positive role models for children in lesbian families

- ▼ blocks both parents in lesbian couples to be named as legal parents (except in states where the second parent can adopt)

- ▼ excludes us from socializing as couples and families with other couples and families from our work places, religious organizations and community groups

- ▼ invalidates our relationships and families, making representation of our needs very difficult in local and national political arenas

What is to be done about this? Good news. There are paths out of the tar pits and antidotes to the goo's effects. Here they are.

- ▼ Tell the truth about who we are as lesbians, where we can, and as often as we can.

- ▼ Support, encourage and accept each other in that truth-telling.

- ▼ Remember that we don't define or represent each other.

- Create safe places to socialize, find and enjoy each other — events, support groups, sports, child-care networks, social clubs, professional clubs, service organizations, lesbian and gay chapters of established organizations (such as the Sierra Club, the Alumni Association or political parties).

- Establish clear financial and legal agreements with our partners in the ways available to us — wills and durable power of attorney agreements, joint tenancy, and other instructive documentation.

- Create our own rituals and rites of passage — couple and friendship commitments, weddings, acknowledging accomplishments, births, co-parenting, godparent relationships, and memorials.

- Build and maintain supportive extended family and social networks.

- Seek and value friendships with other lesbians and lesbian families.

- Encourage and support our children in dealing with homophobia by validating their challenges and modeling openness and positive self-esteem.

- Take political action in the ways that fit for each of us — writing letters to representatives, contributing time, effort, and/or money to candidates who support lesbian/gay rights, join activist groups like Queer Nation and The Human Rights Campaign.

- Educate others about our lack of rights on an individual basis.

- Pursue redress when our legal rights have been violated.

- Love ourselves and one another in the best ways we know.

The author clearly encourages coming out *when possible* for the sake of individual health and sanity with an accompanying benefit of social change. I realize that each individual's choices affect a relationship in it's entirety, given the complex challenges inherent to that process. Differences in needs and circumstances mean that there will be tension involved in these choices. This process will be addressed in the next chapter.

Addictions

Addictive behavior short-circuits skillful relating. It is a coping mechanism developed to deal with emotional or physical pain. This includes addictions to substances such as alcohol or drugs, and to behaviors such as compulsive spending, eating, doing, talking, working and gambling. These coping mechanisms become self-destructive. Any addictive process interferes with one's ability to feel, think clearly and relate honestly or intimately over time.

Mismatched, Outmoded or Underdeveloped Emotional Skills

One of the major barriers to lasting relationships is the a lack of personal skills. Immaturity, self-centeredness, poor boundaries and insensitivity are just a few deterrents to good relating. Of course, none of us is perfect, but there are positive personal goals to strive for.

Brave Hearts Will Out

While challenges to lasting lesbian relationship are real, they rarely outweigh our natural desire and inclination for sharing our lives with another. These barriers may be large in numbers, but perseverance, creativity, an open mind and a kind heart will prevail.

Chapter 4

Personal Skills

*"You gain strength, courage and confidence by every experience
which you must stop and look fear in the face...
You must do the thing you think you cannot do."*
ELEANOR ROOSEVELT

Now that you've looked at some of the challenges to sustaining that "love of your life" you may ask yourself if it's even possible? Sometimes relationship is a complex juggling act of issues and concerns, but other times it's like a sweet ride down a gentle river. Don't be discouraged, after all there is a tremendous positive reward.

The Skills and Abilities You Need

The following personal abilities allow for strong, meaningful relationships. The ones that we most need are the ones that take a great deal of individual effort. More often than not we choose a partner that requires us to develop the very abilities we lack.

Autonomy is a sense of oneself as a separate individual. It includes the ability to do things on one's own in a way that is fulfilling. It means being self-governing. If you are caught up in your partner to the extent that you lose your sense of independence, you are no longer contributing to the partnership. Autonomy carried to the extreme is emotional distance and disconnectedness. This is just as destructive to a relationship as lack of autonomy.

Maturity is having a perspective that goes beyond one's own world and experiences. It means balancing rational thought and emotion and having the willingness to put aside immediate gratification of needs when necessary. It means having tolerance for being misunderstood. The extreme of Emotional Maturity is stuffiness and the inability to play.

Self-awareness has many layers. How often do you spend time contemplating the state of your being? Are you aware of feelings that come up moment to moment? Do you know what your

defensive patterns are? How are you influenced by your work and family? Are you aware of your body? Do you notice when you're full, tired or out of balance? When things get heated we tend to lose sight of what's really going on inside. Anger can cover feelings of hurt or fear. Hyperactivity can cover feelings of sorrow or depression. The more we know about ourselves the better able we are to deal with others fairly and consciously. The extreme of self-awareness is self-absorption or narcissism.

Ability to take responsibility for your behavior, your choices and your shortcomings. It helps if we can accept that we all make bad decisions, or act out at times. We all have character defects. Acknowledging this is not an excuse for continueing to behave badly, but is a step towards setting goals for ourselves that will improve our actions and consequently our self-esteem. Focusing on your own self improvement (instead of hers) makes a huge difference in succesful relationships. In order to do this you must struggle to stay out of shame. Shame is a destructive state of mind that feels humiliating and interferes with our ability to think clearly or act rationally.

Sensitivity to others is a learnable skill that involves paying attention to verbal and nonverbal cues others give. By paying attention to these things you can recognize other peoples emotional states and respond accordingly. By putting yourself in someone elses shoes, imagining what they are going through emotionally, you can develop empathy. Empathy is a fundamental emotional skill that allows us to connect deeply with another person. The extreme of sensitivity to others is excessive worrying and caretaking, or chronic second-guessing.

Ability to communicate clearly requires the ability to detach, to listen, to reveal and to be assertive. This is so important that Chapter 8, *Speaking Up*, is devoted entirely to it.

Ability to manage your emotional distress requires that you know what soothes you when you are upset, anxious or angry and then using that knowledge to help you calm down or disengage if necessary, from a destructive situation. (See Appendix B.)

Though you may possess many of these personal skills, your skills may clash with hers. For example, you may be sensitive to others but unaware of your own feelings. She may be extremely self-aware but not tuned in to your needs. You feel slighted and ignored; she feels you're too intrusive and needy. Neither of these perceptions is necessarily true, but there can be hurt feelings nonetheless. A key to untangling this knot lies in understanding the meanings her behaviors have for you. Our perceptions give words and behaviors meaning. It may be useful to hear what your partner's perceptions are as well, but it's essential to start with your own.

Difficulty arises when old skills learned in families and past relationships no longer work. Suddenly they are backfiring. You may have learned a certain way of communicating that was very indirect. In your family it got you what you wanted without making anyone mad, so you unconsciously continue doing it. Your partner, however, gets angry with your indirect suggestions or implications, and you feel that she's downright rude when she speaks directly in an effort to get her way. Learning each others histories, where these assumptions and interpretations come from, can add an element of compassion and tolerance to these exchanges. Self-awareness of these assumptions can allow for the choice to change them.

Differentiation

All of the above personal skills are part of developing what is called differentiation. Differentiation is the ability to stay emotionally connected to another person while holding onto yourself and what's important to you — without speeding towards agreement or withdrawal — while under stress. Differentiation allows us to engage in conflict without breaking connection to the other and to be inter-dependent without losing ourselves. A well-

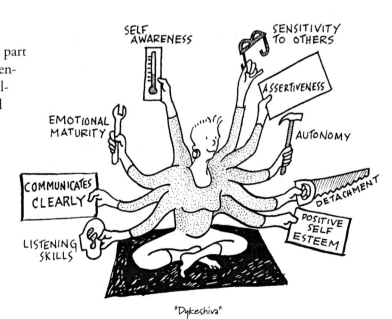

"Dykeshiva"

differentiated person can accept differences and also be willing to change without a threat to their identity.

It involves the active, ongoing process of self-exploration, understanding and self-definition — and managing any anxiety that comes from what you find about yourself — then being able to express important aspects of yourself to your partner in a responsible manner. It is the ability to maintain one's boundaries and manage any anxiety that comes from risking either separation or intimacy. And it is the ability to be curious about your partner's self-disclosure while managing your own reactions.

The Tasks Involved in Differentiation

▾ Commit yourself to an active, ongoing process of self-exploration, understanding and self-definition, and to managing any anxiety that comes from what you find.

▾ Develop the ability to identify and express important aspects of yourself (feelings, thoughts, desires, beliefs, etc.).

▾ Activate yourself towards individual goals that will make you a fuller, happier person. It's easy to know how we want the other person to change, but goals set for ourselves alone are much more effective.

▾ Develop the ability to control the expression of your emotions — so that a thinking capacity remains available under stress.

▾ Develop the ability to calm yourself in order to maintain a non-anxious presence in the face of another person's anxiety. Become non-reactive to the other's reactivity. If one person remained non-reactive many conflicts would not escalate into hurtful fights.

▾ Maintain your boundaries and manage the anxiety that comes from risking separation.

▾ Maintain connection and manage the anxiety that comes from risking intimacy. Be curious about your partner's self-disclosure while managing your own reactions.

▾ Develop the ability to stay connected emotionally, while holding onto yourself and what's important to you — without speeding towards agreement or withdrawal — while under stress.

All of the exercises in this book are related to developing these personal skills *and* to helping you recognize that connection and interdependance are healthy and necessary for secure loving relationships.

Chapter 5

Beyond Dating

*"The flip side to being attracted to unavailable people is
how bored you are by available people. Available people are terrifying
because they want to hang around long enough to know you, to like
you, to accept you. The problem is not that you attract unavailable
people — the problem is that you give them your number."*

MARIANNE WILLIAMSON

Finding a Good Match

Some factors increase chances for relationship success and other factors just don't matter. We may not use the same criteria as our parents, but the intent is the same — to find a good match. The following can help in this endeavor.

How Intimate Do You Want to Be?

Do you both want a similar level of intimacy? A serious mis-match in this area usually results in misery. Long-term struggle and agonizing endings can be drawn…way…out.

Here is an example of people with differing ideas about what they want. Do any of these situations sound familiar?

You have stars in your eyes for her, but she considers you to be the best bowling buddy ever. She gazes lovingly at the woman she sees daily in the elevator who is friendly, but reserved. The "elevator wonder" is in her third year of trying to decide whether or not to cut off a frustrating affair with a married woman who is always "almost ready" to divorce her husband and make a commitment. Meanwhile, you've consistently turned down dates for coffee from the talented woman in your judo class.

Enduring relationships, be they gratifying or frustrating, don't last unless the level of intimacy each person wants is compatible. The level of involvement is usually determined by the person who wants the least intimacy. If the more interested woman persists and the less interested woman changes her mind, it may work, but there are no guarantees of a change of mind. Therefore, the first criterion for "good partnership material" is a commonly desired level of intimacy.

We experience differing levels of intimacy with different people. One level is not more desirable than the others, yet each has its requirements, effects and benefits. Terence T. Gorski, a specialist in treating adult children of alcoholics, lists the five levels of intimacy below.

Levels of Intimacy[1]

Casual: An acquaintance, i.e., neighbor, newsstand person, co-workers.

Companion: A commonly enjoyed activity is the focus, i.e., kayaking, sci-fi movies.

Friend: Relating with the person is the focus and activity comes second; emotional intimacy.

Romantic: Friendship with sexual intimacy; term of "lover."

Partnership: Friendship, romance, and long-term commitment; collaborative efforts and projects; mutual concern regarding relationship and another's well-being.

Levels of intimacy increase as you progress through the stages of relationships. (See Chapter 7, *Cycles of Long Term Relationships*, for a detailed discussion.) Often, zooming from superficial to intense involvement, leaping from acquaintanceship into partnership, results in a wicked case of emotional whiplash and possible dissolution of the relationship.

EXERCISE 5 — *Categorizing Your Friends*   ♀/♀♀

1. Referring to the above description of five levels of intimacy, identify a person in your life who fits each level.

---

1 Terence Gorski, *Getting Love Right, Learning the Choices of Healthy Intimacy*, Fireside/Parkside Recovery Press, N.Y., 1993, pg. 204.

Emotional Maturity

The desire for intimacy does not guarantee that we have the ability to attain it. Emotional maturity is a necessity, and it includes some of these elements:

- tolerance for being misunderstood
- ability to exercise impulse control and experience delayed gratification
- owning and expressing feelings, intentions and mistakes
- acknowledging the effects one's actions have on others
- empathy for others' experiences

EXERCISE 6 — Rate Your Emotional Maturity   ♀

Using a scale of 0 to 10, with 0 equaling "none" and 10 equaling "sainthood," rate yourself in each of the areas below.

NOW	5 YEARS AGO	
_____	_____	tolerance of being misunderstood
_____	_____	impulse control and delayed gratification
_____	_____	owning and expressing feelings, intentions and mistakes
_____	_____	acknowledging the effects one's actions have on others
_____	_____	empathy for others' experiences

Track Record

If you want to know something about how someone will relate in the future, look at what they've done in the past. While people do grow and change for the better, a persons' history is still a good source of information regarding strengths and weaknesses. Listen to what she's telling you about herself. Don't let the state of infatuation garble your perception.

Physical Health

Physical health also determines how available one is for a relationship. Active addictions — be they process addictions such as gambling, co-dependence, sex and love, and/or workaholism, or substance addictions such as alcoholism or other drug additions — severely limit one's capacity to create and sustain relationships at any level of intimacy.

Other major health concerns do not have to block healthy relating. However, these need to be made known early in a relationship. Physical disabilities, hidden or otherwise, can play a role in availability. Realistic acknowledgment can prevent unrealistic expectations and will build trust.

Any health concern that poses a threat to the other person needs to be made known before it is a threat, e.g., venereal disease, herpes, being HIV positive. Timing is crucial and a sensitive concern. It is not necessary to lead with such information as, "Hi, my name's Suzanne and I have vaginal warts. What's your name?" However, if you're about to be physically intimate and expose this wonderful new person to something not so wonderful, it's time to be verbally intimate. Talk about it. (See *Dating*, page 12–14, for more on safe sex issues.)

Proximity

Have you ever been attracted to, developed a crush on, or fallen in love with someone you met from another city? State? Country? If so, proximity becomes a major factor. If long-distance relationships are an unsatisfying pattern for you and yours, you may benefit from looking at the hidden reasons that make it attractive. Distance naturally limits the consistent intimacy possible and the degree of involvement. If that works for you, hey, there's no need to fix what isn't broken. If doesn't work for you, then try dating closer to home — or moving your home!

Enjoyment of the Person

Emotional maturity, relationship track records, physical health and proximity all determine how available we are. Even if all of these check out as A-OK, genuine enjoyment of the other person is a must. Liking each other's company is a basic necessity if you want to continue past dating to being a couple. Here's where personal tastes and preferences hold their full, subjective sway.

Interests and Values

Common interests and values help at first, and if they are not readily apparent, they can be developed. It doesn't matter if your friends think you're mismatched — the question is, do you enjoy each other? Shared interests don't absolutely make or break a relationship, but commonalties can make rough times much easier.

EXERCISE 7 — Shared and Unshared Interests and Values   ♀

1. List those interests and values you and your intended (or partner) share.

2. List those you will need to pursue on your own or with another friend.

When Does Dating Become More Than Dating?

With amazing frequency, a strange thing begins to happen somewhere along the dating path. You find someone with whom you want more than an evening at the movies or dinner and dancing at the bistro. You still want that, of course, but now you begin to think of staying home together and peeling potatoes in front of the TV. Maybe you're the type who likes to find her underwear mixed up with yours in the hamper. You find that you enjoy having your names linked in conversation and take pride in being seen with her. You tire of schlepping your suitcase back and forth from her place to yours. Visions of vacations together fill your head, and the advantages of sharing the rent/mortgage seem ever so practical. If you have ever had these or similar thoughts, then you are dangerously close to dealing with the issues of commitment and something known as defining the relationship. Notice that, suddenly, dating has become "something else." This "something else" can strike terror into the hearts of the strong and brave, or it can bring relief, security and comfort.

"Commitment" is a word with many applications. You are committed to having dinner tonight. You are committed to being honest. You are committed to feeding your dog. These different kinds of commitments

37

require varied degrees of effort and follow-through. But overall, commitment means a strong desire and intention to follow through on something.

In a relationship, there are many points along the way where commitments are made. These are often made automatically, or unconsciously. It is best to stay conscious of these changes and, yes, even to talk about them! As you talk about the changes, your assumptions and ideas can be explored. At some point the idea of making the commitment to becoming a "couple" is likely to come up. Your definitions of a couple may differ and it is important to share that with each other as these affect current and future expectations.

What Defines You as a "Couple"?

Cultural and family influences dictate many of our assumptions about what defines a couple. Awareness of these assumptions is important. As you read the next section, mentally note which of these assumptions or views you hold, or would like to hold, in your relationship.

Independent Decision Making vs. Joint Decision Making

As a single person, our decisions are our own. When we become a couple we have a lot more collaboration to do as our decisions effect each other. Small, everyday choices don't always matter and can be cumbersome to discuss, but other decisions such as what to do with our funds, our job, or our time do matter.

Commitment to a relationship means commitment to the well-being of another person. Consulting and discussing mutual and separate needs before making decisions is part of that commitment. This is not the same as asking permission from one another. Phrases such as "Would you mind if I...?" or " How do you feel about...?" are considerate ways to include the other. Lest you get peevish, remember that your decisions are your own no matter how strong the input from the outside. It is nevertheless important to open up discussion with your partner so she feels included. However, the big decisions about family, work, and time priorities need to be mutually agreed on (or a compromise worked out) for a true sense of cohesiveness.

Monogamy vs. Polyamory

Monogamy — to be or not to be — that is a basic question of coupledom. Often, this decision is made without discussion and is one of the first to define the relationship as a couple.

There is a strong societal bias for monogamy, as well as practical and personal reasons for such. Even so some couples prefer to have an "open" relationship. Agreeing to be non-monogamous is not a guarantee however that you won't be dealing with difficult feelings when theory is put into practice. To many women being sexual outside of a primary relationship is threatening to their sense of security. Hurt, anger, fear and guilt are typical responses to sex outside a relationship. Talking about it and doing it don't always feel the same.

While most lesbian couples choose monogamy, there are some who swear by polyamory. There are couples that feel enriched and satisfied by maintaining more than one sexual/personal relationship. Congratulations to those women. The more people that are involved in intimate relating, the more needs, boundaries and preferences there are to deal with. It can be a complex challenge which some women are anxious to take on, while others are not. The polyamorous community has experience and suggestions to impart.

The most important aspect of this subject is that monogamy or non-monogamy be mutually agreed upon and livable for both. One way is not necessarily more virtuous than the other, though monogamy is usually more practical.

Introductions

Introducing your beloved to parents and friends is a clear statement of intention. It says, "Here she is, my sweetheart. I hope you approve, or at very least accept her presence." However, due to homophobia, introductions to the family may be a long time coming or may never happen at all. It's possible to introduce your partner without making it clear that she's your lover, and you may choose to volunteer the information when you want them to know. Regardless of whether or not you come out, meeting the friends and relations (particularly the relations) represents a step beyond dating into longer-term hopes and dreams.

Holidays

Holidays, weddings, reunions and family gatherings are another step in the process of transitioning from "just" dating to longer-term coupledom. Do I bring her? Do we go to our separate events? Does this mean I come out? Dealing with these issues and/or planning holidays together is a sure sign that you've moved beyond the dating stage to "something else."

Presents

Giving presents can be another sign of coupledom. You're past the point of the flowers or the occasional dinner and movie treat. Now you find yourself eyeing clothes that would just look great on her; you have the urge to get her the placemats that match her kitchen tiles. Everywhere you look there is another object crying out to you, "Pick me! She'll love me!" Gift giving also tends to bring up issues of material values, of obligation, reciprocity and differing financial resources, so be aware of the effect it has.

Rings, "Going Steady" Jewelry, Matching Haircuts

Outward manifestations of love and mutual involvement can be charming and richly symbolic. Rings have a history that dates back to pagan times when youths who were entering the service of the Goddess became wedded to Venus. Other types of "going steady" jewelry such as I.D. bracelets, pins, and lockets are of a more recent vintage. Matching clothing, jewelry and hairstyle are customs that seem to have been born directly from the loins of the lesbian community. (The research data isn't complete.)

Getting "Married" — Public or Private Ceremonies

Rituals and ceremonies have always been used to signify important passages, and the passage from singlehood to coupledom is important indeed. Being outside tradition does have its advantages. It means more flexibility in choosing ceremonies and fewer parental expectations to fulfill. We can do it just about any old way we please. Go for it — wear the gown with the cowgirl boots or the tux with the veil (just make it easy on yourself — call the caterer).

Demanding the choice to marry is claiming the rights and responsibilities of full citizenship. The historically patriarchal underpinnings of marriage can be transformed into more liberating forms of partnership. What to call this event and what it means has been a hotly debated item among the species of lesbiana politicalus. Is marriage a patriarchal institution? Is getting married a "wanna-be" cop-out, or is it a bold statement of pride, entitlement and social protest? This debate was hotly contested in the 1980's and 1990's.

The "Right To Marry Movement," is currently going strong. It is a civil rights movement that started in the early 1990's and has gained in strength (and opposition) since. The rights and responsibilities of legalized marriage are far reaching. They include, but are not limited to, rights to joint parenting and adoption, joint child custody, spousal health care insurance, hospital and jail visitation, joint home and auto insurance, widow's survivorship benefits, pensions, tax and immigration benefits, dissolution and divorce protections such as community property and child support, bereavement leave, domestic violence protection orders and others.

At the time of this writing there is no Federally recognized legal marriage for lesbians.. There are inroads in some States however, and recent "Domestic Partnership" agreements instated by specific companies, Cities, Counties, and States bring many of these rights to couples, but certainly not all. Some states are now able to boast state legalized marriage, though this continues to be challenged by the electorate and the courts. The Federal right of lesbians to marry legally would be a tremendous inroad to parity and recognition on many fronts. In the meantime, lesbian "marriages" and rituals, though not often legally enforceable, can be creative and meaningful.

Of course it is a matter of opinion and circumstances that determine the positive and negative aspects of choosing to commit to a legalized partnership, be it a "marriage" license or a domestic partnership contract. There are responsibilities (to assume debt, potential child support or alimony, community property, possible need for pre-nups) as well as the rights listed above. Think well and discuss freely all the implications before making such a life changing decision.

Living Together

For many individuals, being a couple includes living together. Resolving the questions of when to move in and where to live can be a rite of passage itself. Some couples may not include cohabitation in their definition, finding it comfortable and convenient to have separate domiciles.

Pooling Resources

There are many ways to pool resources, depending on the resources and comfort level of each person. "Yours, mine and ours" is another criteria of being a couple. Resources include CDs and books, food, time, chores, special talents, furniture, tools, clothing, household appliances, and, last but not least, money. Money is another area for negotiation and conscious choice.

Co-parenting?

Co-parenting is a large commitment, whether it's sharing responsibility for parenting children from a previous relationship, adopting, or going through the birth experience together. It is a part of being a couple that is desired in the minds of some and not of others. Women with children, or planning to have children, should not take for granted that their prospective partners will want to share equally in the co-parenting process and they should be prepared to explore this area deeply, delving into all assumptions. We recommend a visit to your library for material written on "blended families" if either or both of you bring children into the relationship.

How About "Co-petting"?

And then there are the pets. Though you never thought it would come to this, you're now refilling the water bowl and splitting the vet bill. "Co-petting" is something that many find themselves doing. A pet is often a lesbian's best friend. Pets can serve as substitute children, members of the family. To those animal lovers out there, you know what a true sacrifice it is to ask Bowser to give up his special place on the bed. What if you both have pets? "Blended" families provide a myriad of challenges (particularly inter-species families.) All relationships involve some sacrifice. If you're willing to compromise here, it is a sure sign that you're a couple.

Wills, Power-of-Attorney, Adoption, Living Trusts

Given the absence of legal protection for lesbian couples by current law and custom, we must maximize the benefits and rights available to us. One way to do this is to set up legal documents to protect ourselves. This includes the right to have one's lover/partner make health care decisions if you are incapacitated (Power-of-Attorney for Health Care), to ensure that your children and partner remain intact as a family if anything should happen to you (Second Parent Adoption or Guardianship), and to allow you to inherit or leave property if you or your partner should die (Wills or Living Trusts). These contracts are essential protections, particularly if children and joint property are involved. They are also tangible symbols of commitment to the longevity of the relationship. (At this writing, when adoption is denied for a non-biological lesbian co-parent, there is no legal protection — so be very clear about this risk.)

While heterosexuals have the legal system for dealing with divorce, unless we are legally "Registered Domestic Partners," or have the good fortune to have state legislation, we have to wing it when we split up. In some cases this may be beneficial, allowing us to be kinder and more creative. However, kindness is not always the emotion of the day when hurt feelings and disappointments abound. It is a good idea to have prior agreements in place to help you and your partner handle things fairly should there be the dissolution of the relationship. These legal written agreements lead to peace of mind even when there is absolutely no intention of splitting up.

While I recommend using an attorney versed in gay and lesbian precedent, this is not always financially feasible. There are excellent guidelines for drawing up your own documents at NOLO Press, Berkeley, California (800-728-3555, www.nolo.com).

EXERCISE 8 — *What's a Couple?*   9/9

1. Using the partnership criteria itemized in this chapter (pages 34–38), identify the ones that are important in your definition of being a couple.

2. Consider sharing your answer with your significant other. It could be quite revealing and helpful to you both.

Defining Yourselves

Whether by ceremony, dress, gifts, legal entanglements or checkbooks, you have the option of creating a custom fit. We hope your union fits you to a 't'. Alterations are always possible.

Chapter 6

Coming Out and Being Out

"I will not be just a tourist in the world of images,
just watching images passing by which I cannot live in,
make love to, possess as permanent sources of joy and ecstasy."
ANAÏS NIN

"Straightening Up" the Apartment

"Straightening Up" the Apartment

"Coming out" is a process, not an event. At some point in each lesbian's lifetime, she notices a stirring (no, not there...in the cerebral cortex) different from the stories and pictures, the folklore and gossip about man/woman love and sex. As she pays attention to these feelings about women she finds there are possibilities to explore. And so, coming out begins.

It may take a moment or a day or years to come out to oneself, actually recognizing and, yes, admitting that you "love" other women, or claiming the identity of "Lesbian" or "Bi-sexual." Coming out to others then becomes an issue. We decide each day of our lives whether to come out in some small or large way. We have to answer the questions "where?...how much?...with whom?" when we respond to questions about ourselves, or are confronted with heterosexual assumptions. And we have to do it over and over and over. Coming out can be a small risk or a huge risk, rarely comfortable, often liberating, sometimes disastrous, but certainly important.

Where to Come Out

Most of us are only comfortable being "out" in certain areas of our lives. Different levels of intimacy exist with different individuals and groups of people, so it is logical that some people will know us better than others and coming out will be done selectively. However, partners' conflicting ideas about "being out" can cause relationship problems; for example, one may feel comfortable being out at work while the other may feel just the opposite.

Introducing Mel and Di

Dinah and Melody introduce themselves at their initial couples' counseling appointment. Dinah is mid-30ish. She is engaging and friendly, dressed in jeans, a tailored vest and a silk blouse. Melody is in her late 20's, with close-cropped blonde hair. She appears more reserved, yet comfortable, in her cords, sweater and black boots. They have been lovers and have lived together for several years. Until recently they have considered their relationship satisfying. The frequency and intensity of their conflicts have become of such significant concern they have sought counseling. They list feeling untrusting, increasing despair and are increasingly unable to effectively talk to each other.

Melody relates a recent disagreement about emergency plumbing repairs undertaken on the home they co-own. Dinah explains, *"The hot water heater was gushing all over the back porch. We were in complete agreement about calling a plumber. We even agreed how to select someone — we have a warranty plan, and it's essentially whoever they send out. So we don't know who we're going to get — they could be a member of the Aryan Nation for all I know — which*

46

is where we really disagree. I'm not comfortable being out to someone I don't know. You never know what they'll do when you come out to them. Coming out could be dangerous. I know. I've had serious consequences come from being out. I need to check out who they are first."

Melody interrupts: *"You mean you need to know their birth date, their political party, and what their favorite color is. If you had it your way, neither of us would be out to anyone unless we'd known them for ages. I can't live that way. Besides, it's vital that every lesbian be out. Otherwise, homophobia will never change."*

Each woman has a different degree of comfort with being out. It is determined by their differing personalities and past experiences. They're not really aware of the emotional needs that are being met by these differing positions but they will passionately advocate for them nonetheless. Further discussion revealed that they actually do have many values and interests in common, however, their ideas of where, how much, when, and whom to come out to are in conflict. Melody feels most comfortable with expressing her sexual identity up front with whomever she meets. The other person's receptivity or defensiveness lets her know if this is someone she can trust in business, friendship or elsewhere. Dinah needs to get to know someone before she feels safe enough to disclose her sexual identity. She needs to interact with them and be reassured that the person is relatively non-homophobic before she entrusts them with what she considers privileged information.

The means by which each woman creates safety for herself is mutually exclusive to her partner's method and is thereby perceived as inherently threatening.

Each woman has found her particular approach effective for her. Each thinks it is a necessary response, given the risks of living in a homophobic world. They clearly share the same goal, yet their methods clash. What can they do? Before leaping into possible solutions, check out what you and your sweetheart have in common or in contrast with Mel and Di.

Exercise 9 — Different Outs for Different Folks ♀

1. Where do you feel most comfortable being out?

2. Where do you feel least comfortable being out?

Pause & Reflect

3. What effect does this have on your relationship?

How Much Do You Want to Be Out?

Melody's choice of dress, hair and her nickname, "Mel," automatically makes her appear more stereotypically lesbian. Dinah's self-presentation leaves her the task and the option of coming out in conversation or actions.

How much to be out is a decision we each make every day. Some women are naturally at ease with dress and manner that might convey their lesbianism. For them comfort in dress and their unique style comes before social convention. Other women are more comfortable in attire, or with behavior that doesn't imply lesbianism. Each woman, regardless of her intent, gets responses based on other people's assumptions and perceptions. When partners have different comfort levels and ways of being out, conflict — and possible growth — can result.

The heart of Dinah's and Mel's conflict involves the "when," "whom" and "how" of coming out. Each wants to be able to exercise her own choice and fears losing that choice if she accommodates her partner's needs. Getting clearer about their respective assumptions and fears about these coming out decisions can help them determine possible resolutions.

Do you feel more comfortable coming out to others from the beginning so they know you are lesbian and you can observe their responses, as Mel does?

Are you similar to Dinah, who prefers getting to know someone and building a relationship before coming out?

How do you and/or your partner approach coming out?

EXERCISE 10 — Comparing Outs   ♀/♀♀

Answer these questions individually first. When you're clear with yourself, compare and discuss your answers with your partner.

1. How do you communicate being out?

2. How are you and your partner different in being out? How are you similar?

3. What do you like about your partner's ways of being out? What do you dislike?

4. How do you usually deal with differences between your lover and yourself concerning coming out? *Pause & Reflect*

When to Come Out

When to come out is a question that can make the difference between an awkward situation, a dangerous one, or a "successful" experience. Success is determined by the expectations and assumptions one begins with. Timing isn't everything, but it is something.

- ▾ Do I say it now, at the family's annual holiday party when everyone is feeling especially generous?

- ▾ Do I wait until Aunt Julia's wedding when I want to bring a "guest"?

- ▾ Do I let my co-workers know right off so they don't make assumptions and remarks, or do I wait until they know me first?

EXERCISE 11 — *Coming-Out Time Bombs* ♀/♀♀

Answer these questions individually first. When you're clear, compare and discuss your answers with each other.

1. Recall the worst timing you've had in a coming-out experience. What made it the worst?

2. As a general rule, do you come out to someone if you've known them a day, a week, a month, a year? What is your sense of comfortable timing?

Who Should You Come Out To?

Who is safe? We usually try to come out first to someone we think is going to be supportive or at least kind. This could be another gay person, a bisexual or straight friend, or a relative. Often, we progress to those who are more risky after testing the waters and our own resolve.

- ▼ "Is Mom/Dad really ready to hear this?" (Or more to the point, am I ready to deal with her/his response?)

- ▼ "I can't stand the thought of going to work and pretending to be single and "het" one more day. I'm going to tell Jean at the front desk. She's someone I can be myself with."

EXERCISE 12 — Bull's-Eye   ♀/♀♀

---

1. Take a piece of paper and write the word "me" in the center. Draw concentric circles around it (like a bull's-eye). Place the initials of those people you are closest to emotionally in the closest circle, the next level of intimacy in the next circle, and so on, until you have the initials of the key players in your life in your picture. Include family, people from work, social circles, spiritual/religious groups.

2. Now, circle the initials of everyone you are out to.

3. Step back from your work and take in all that information. How does it strike you? Is there anything about this picture you would like to change?

4. Share this exercise and your feelings about it with someone you trust.

How Long Have You Been Out?

The length of time you've been out is an important factor in your comfort level. It can influence your choice of partners or your compatibility with a partner. Of course, the length of time is a subjective matter, depending on the point of demarcation. How do you mark your coming out?

- ▼ your first experience of attraction or being in love

- ▼ your first sexual encounter with another woman

- ▾ telling your parent(s) of your feelings for women

- ▾ going to your first gay event

In the course of couple's counseling, Mel's and Di's therapist asked each of them to relate their individual coming out histories. She asked when they first realized they were attracted to women; how and when they first disclosed this information to others; and how they first identified other lesbians. Mel began.

"I always knew I was more like the boys in my family and neighborhood than the girls. I knew I wasn't a boy, but I liked the things boys liked — sports, being outdoors, riding my bike fast over dirt hills, building forts, that kind of thing. I was never comfortable or interested in the usual girl clothes. So it didn't seem so odd to me when I realized I liked girls the same way most boys liked girls. But I didn't think about it all that much until I was old enough for most of my friends to start dating. At thirteen I got this incredible crush on my best friend's older sister. My buddy Daaron and his sixteen-year-old sister, Sharon, lived across the street. I was smitten bad. All I wanted to do was hang out at Daaron's house to see if Sharon was going to be around. Then I would tease her mercilessly in what I considered to be a very witty and casual manner. Daaron saw right through me and said that if I wanted to hang around the house all of the time it was my business but he was going out to find someone who wanted to do something. I was mortified and torn. I made the big mistake of telling my mom how gorgeous I thought Sharon was. My mom got all happy and said she'd be glad to take me shopping so we could get some "outfits" like Sharon wore. I was embarrassed and miserable, but after much nagging I agreed to go with her. I hated everything she suggested. I was really obnoxious and we ended up in a screaming match in the car on the way home. My mom cried. I felt horrible because I knew she was only trying to help. I vowed then never to pretend to be different than who I am, regardless of who does or doesn't get it."

Di had heard only part of this story and not in the context of Mel's coming out. She felt a lot of empathy and compassion for her conflicted and misunderstood lover. Next Dinah told her story.

"I came to the awareness of my sexual identity much later in life than Melody did. My brother and I spent most of our years growing up outside the United States. My father was part of the diplomatic corps in the foreign service and we lived in Belgium and later in Greece. My mother left teaching when I was born and returned to it when my younger brother went off to school. I felt comfortable with being a girl and I was very concerned with doing everything the right way. My family emphasized appropriate behavior at all times. It was crucial to avoid offending anyone and not embarrass our parents, particularly my dad. I became diligent and skillful in scanning whatever situ-

ation I was in to determine who was who, and what was expected from me. In grade school I attended coed classes with other kids whose families were in the foreign service or were American military personnel. When I was a teenager, my father was assigned to Greece and I attended an all-girls school through graduation.

I had always had one very close girlfriend — somewhat like serial monogamy, only we were just friends. Those relationships were defined as platonic, although in my early teens my girlfriends and I had many slumber parties where the behavior was quite sexual. We used to "practice" kissing and slow dancing with each other. I would only "practice" with my best friend, whereas the other girls kissed and danced with everyone at the party. They all seemed just as interested in eating junk food, watching monster movies and gossiping. All I wanted to do was practice kissing and slow dancing. I felt ashamed and tried to hide my interest in those activities.

I came back to the United States to attend college. It wasn't until then that I realized my closest friendships with some women were more than platonic. I got incredibly jealous when my current best friend dated or did things with other people. Other women friends could do the same thing and it wouldn't faze me.

When I was a sophomore I read one of those lesbian paperbacks, the ones with the racy covers. I would never have bought one, but one was being passed around our dorm and my roommate gave it to me because she said I studied too much and should read more trash. The two main characters were college girls who lived in a sorority house and were lovers. I felt like I'd been hit by lightning. I couldn't put the book down, which mortified me and meant I had to hide it behind my French literature books for fear anyone could tell how riveted I was. I found it incredibly arousing. Ninety percent of the characters' feelings could have been mine, except I wasn't lovers with anyone.

There were actually several girls in that dorm pegged as "homo." I ended up as a lab partner in chemistry with one of them. I was so anxious I kept knocking things over. I felt intimidated and so conflicted. I didn't want to become labeled as "one of them," yet I was totally fascinated. She was great. She didn't act like she noticed a thing except to suggest one time, after I had knocked over a rack of test tubes, that I lay off caffeine on lab days. She was very funny, after I caught on that the majority of her comments were not to be taken seriously. She hardly ever cracked a smile but she had the most articulate wit. We got to be pretty good friends. She and her lover took me to my first lesbian bar when I turned twenty-one the next year. I became a regular and who should I meet there a month or so later but my dorm-mate from the previous year. She actually introduced me to my first "official" woman lover."

Give yourselves the opportunity to learn more of how the coming out process weaves through your life and other lesbian's lives using these next questions. You may already have shared much of this information with each other, but there is always a new perspective uncovered by reviewing personal histories. Exchanging such history allows for more understanding and empathy for each other then and now.

Some stories are painful, some are silly, some are fun or touching. All are part of our personal heritage and lesbian experience.

EXERCISE 13 — Coming Out — Out Loud   ♀/♀♀

1. To acquaint yourself further with the variety of experiences in coming out (and enjoy yourself while doing so), try reading from the book *The Original Coming Out Stories*, edited by Julia Penelope and Susan J. Wolfe (Crossing Press, Inc., 1989). Do this on your own, or, if you like, read it to your partner or friend. You may be surprised at how diverse and how similar coming out experiences are.

2. Set aside some time to tell coming out stories. They make for great dinner or party conversations.
   ▾ If you are in a relationship, set aside a time to tell each other your own stories.
   ▾ Ask your friends to tell you theirs.
   ▾ Have a "coming out party" and ask for a coming out story from each guest as a party game.

Considering Homophobia

HOMOPHOBIA, noun: (American Heritage Dictionary)
    1. Fear, dislike or hatred of gay men and lesbians.
    2. Discrimination against lesbians and gay men.

You can't talk about coming out without including the topic of homophobia. It has a pervasive impact on our lives as lesbians, both as individuals and in relationship. Much of this book would not be necessary if homophobia didn't exist. When people fear others and feel threatened by differences, hatred and discrimination result. Though they are not healthy, homophobic and oppressive ideas and behaviors remain the cultural norm.

Differences in human sexuality are perceived by many cultures as taboo. Other differences in human behavior such as left-handedness vs. right-handedness are not reasons for condemnation and rejection. This genetically carried characteristic is not perceived as threatening or deviant. It is not spoken of in hushed tones or in the privacy of one's home. Left-handedness hasn't always been so accepted, however. It was common practice in grade schools in the United States as recently as the 1950s for teachers to require left-handed children to write only with their right hands to try to make them conform to the majority. Being a lesbian is still widely considered threatening and deviant.

Homophobia comes in many shapes, flavors and packages. Some homophobia comes with a big bright label marked: "We hate gays." That's overt homophobia. Covert homophobia looks benign and shows its ugliness only upon closer inspection. We live with both the obvious (overt) and the subtle (covert) forms. We carry it deep inside, knowingly or not. Our culture is homophobic and being raised as a part of that culture we are not immune to it's influence.

One of the essential elements of good self-esteem is the ability to be genuine. Homophobia creates a double-bind regarding self-esteem. When we express our true selves we are at risk of homophobic reactions. Negative reactions to expressions of our true selves are limiting and corrosive to self-esteem.

Examples of Overt Homophobia

- ▼ job discrimination

- ▼ name-calling, gay-baiting

- ▼ violent acts against lesbians, gay bashing

- ▼ negative labels

- ▼ loss of friendships or family

- ▼ being taken out of a will

- ▼ not being allowed to visit the nieces or nephews

- ▼ losing custody of children

- ▼ being denied visits to your lover in the hospital because visits are allowed by "family only"

- ▼ having people physically pull away or avoid you when near

- ▼ same-sex couples being denied the option of legal marriage

- ▼ denial of inclusion in the military if declared lesbian or gay

Examples of Covert Homophobia

- ▼ being passed over for promotions at work with no apparent reason
- ▼ being excluded from work-related social functions
- ▼ being rejected from job interviews for no apparent reason
- ▼ being placed on shifts or given only duties with low public profile
- ▼ others presuming that you are straight
- ▼ others feeling sorry for you because you don't have a man
- ▼ only heterosexual couples being represented in ads, TV programs, books, films
- ▼ no one inquiries about your partner or what the two of you have been doing lately

These and other consequences of being out or closeted affect us as individuals and are an additional burden to our relationships.

The support and camaraderie of close relationships with our lovers, friends and community are wonderful and necessary remedies to homophobia. Communication, acceptance and understanding do help limit it's negative effects. These may not be forthcoming from the culture at large, but we can practice them among ourselves.

Homophobic behaviors from others create shame in two ways: by the negative reactions we receive and by the positives that are withheld. Many cultural "goodies" don't come our way as lesbian couples. Their absence is corrosive to self-esteem and the general well-being of our relationships.

These goodies may include:

- ▼ recognized rituals and rites of passage such as weddings and anniversaries
- ▼ wedding presents (including money)
- ▼ legal protection
- ▼ tax breaks
- ▼ health and life insurance
- ▼ family encouragement and interest
- ▼ positive representation in the media
- ▼ military service

Internalized Homophobia

As stated before, it is impossible for each and every one of us not to internalize some cultural homophobic beliefs and fears. Our task is to recognize this and identify our internalized homophobia and its effects on our lives and the people we love. We need to be gentle and forgiving of ourselves while being honest and determined to transform these fears into self-loving and affirming beliefs.

Examples of Internalized Homophobia:

- feeling shame regarding your or your partner's body

- believing deep down that being sexual with another woman is perverse, dirty or wrong

- not wanting to be seen with your partner because she looks too "dykey"

- feeling that you are different from (read "better than") all those other lesbians

- feeling that something is wrong with you, that you should be "normal"

- not wanting the kids to find out that you're gay because: it will upset them; it will change your relationship; "I don't want them to become gay; I don't want them to become ashamed of me"

- feeling critical of or embarrassed by others who choose to be more out than you, or out in different ways than you

- being afraid to touch gays/lesbians and/or members of the same sex

Exercise 14 — Homophobia Stories   ♀/♀♀

---

1. Swap stories with your partner about when you've dealt with homophobia. Trade off on listening and speaking with each other.

   When you're the listener, do not interrupt.

As the speaker, include a description of the feelings that accompanied each experience and include how you presently feel.

2. Identify positive messages that you would have liked to experience in the past. Identify positive messages that you would like to hear now from others. Exchange these positive messages with each other.

EXERCISE 15 — Self-Identify Internalized Homophobia   ♀/♀♀

1. Identify your own homophobic feelings and responses.

2. Describe your own homophobic feelings and responses to your partner and then listen as she describes hers.

EXERCISE 16 — Validating Your Relationship   ♀

Give some thought to these questions.

1. How do you positively validate your relationship?

2. Are there other ways you'd like to validate it?

Pause & Reflect

3. Does homophobia play a part in any ambivalence or hesitation to do these? How?

4. Are there ways you could be more validating and still be comfortable?

The dominant culture is not only fearful of us but is also ashamed of us. It is easy to internalize this shame. How many have had the experience of being called a "queer" or hearing boys being called "faggot" in grade school? Remember how shameful this felt?

Emotional and mental health are strengthened by moving from shame-based beliefs to self-acceptance and acceptance by others.

Though each of us can enjoy our lives in spite of disapproval from others, acceptance remains an important factor in our self-esteem and sense of worth. As a species we are interdependent by nature. We learn from our social environment and depend on feedback for knowledge about ourselves. No woman is an island. We benefit from creating and seeking out supportive environments. We benefit from creating safe and stable connections.

Living from a shame-based perspective creates many effects in a relationship. Some are obvious and some are subtle. When a person is steeped in shame, it is difficult to know or act on one's true preferences. For example, you are invited to a family holiday gathering. You want to go and would like to take your lover. You don't feel comfortable "passing" as straight or pretending you are not a couple, yet if you were "out," the likelihood of strong homophobic reactions from family members would be unpleasant. You consider going by yourself, but you want to celebrate the holiday with your partner. You both don't go.

Mel and Di

Melody and Dinah had their own version of the "holiday dilemma." Melody recalls,

> *"My family always has a large gathering for Thanksgiving. My parents, brothers and sisters and all of our aunts and uncles, cousins and even some family friends get together every year. It's a chaotic affair in some ways. It rotates to different families each year. It's so big we have to use sawhorses with doors laid on them for tables. When I was in high school I thought it was cool to have my own guest. My friends usually liked the whole circus. After I was living on my own there was always a friend or two who were lone strays around Thanksgiving, and I brought them. I also brought my current lover at the time.*

It was a great sorting out test for lovers. If they could stand the noise level and general bedlam of that event, they were probably worth keeping. Dinah did great the first year. That's when she met my family, actually. She loved it! I knew then we were on our way to something serious. We moved in together not long after that.

When, it came around to the second year and I really felt great about us, it hit me that my relationship with Dinah was one of the things I felt most thankful for in my life. So I talked to my mom about Thanksgiving, about how Dinah and I would be coming, and I realized I wanted to make sure everybody knew we were together. All of the people I had brought as guests over the years had always been introduced as friends, whether they were or not. Everybody in my family knew who was a friend or lover (because I had told them at some time). I assume most everybody else did too, but not because of anything I said. People can often just tell. Anyway, I didn't hide that someone was more of a…'date,'…but that's just it, Dinah wasn't just a…'date'…to me anymore and I wanted everybody to know that.

I don't know if my mom understood why this mattered to me so much, she just got that it mattered. She's pretty cool. She thought it was a fine thing to let everybody know and asked me how I wanted to do that. I hadn't gotten that far, but thought I'd talk to Dinah. I imagined that maybe we'd even make some kind of announcement or toast or something for being together for a couple of years, and let everyone know we'd moved in together. My brother and "sister-in-law to be" did that when they had been together a couple of years. I felt really confident and excited about all this and couldn't wait to talk

59

with Dinah. I really thought it would be meaningful to her to know that our relationship was something I was truly thankful for and wanted to acknowledge.

But that's not the way she took it. I should have known. She's cut from a different bolt of cloth. Sometimes our differences can feel really bad. There are lesbians who would give their right arm to have the acceptance my family offers us, but Dinah just pushed it away. I seriously wondered if this relationship was a huge mistake. Being single again looked pretty good. I couldn't stand being with someone who was ashamed of being with me or ashamed of us."

Dinah interrupts.

"I don't really care if everyone else knows we're together, but I couldn't imagine choosing to make ourselves the center of attention to tell them. The whole idea brought on a panic attack. I knew Mel was excited about that Thanksgiving. It was clear that she wanted us to be "out" there that year and that it meant a lot to her, but my stomach got tighter with every word. I felt terrible because I saw how excited Mel was about this. But she is so much more comfortable around groups of people, and this would be with her family and on home turf. Don't get me wrong — I wish I was half as gutsy as she is. She's done an incredible job of being out with her family, and it really shows. She's been out to them for years and assumes they love and accept her as a lesbian, and mostly they do. I knew I just couldn't do it and thought it best not to even try. I could always spend the holiday with other friends or even by myself — that would be so much better, except I knew Mel would be really bummed. I felt ashamed that I couldn't go and do this for her, but I was mortified at the prospect of doing it. We are so different in some ways. I really wish this wasn't such an issue."

Regardless of these hurdles, Melody and Dinah worked out a livable compromise. Information on the specifics of their solution comes later.

Situations worsen when each woman becomes caught in her own reactions of defensiveness and shame. When swept up in defense and shame each woman loses safe connection with her parnter. The conflict becomes a question of whose needs are more important rather than a question of addressing the homophobic pressures in the situation. It is the task of every couple to find a way to link arms and together address dilemmas rather than be separated and polarized as the issue becomes a wedge.

Shame and low self-esteem are very, very close conspirators. To compensate for feeling badly about ourselves, we "people-please" in a zillion ways, including workaholism, being the helpful neighbor, the fixer, the good humor pal, and so on. Such compensating drains time and energy, leaving only meager availability to one's self and relationship. Being too caught up in what others think blocks our knowledge of true needs and desires.

EXERCISE 17 — Identification of Shame   ♀

Remember a situation in which you felt shameful — not guilty of something you did but shameful, (e.g., you were not okay as a person). Recall what secrets or underlying beliefs were attached to this situation. (Underlying beliefs are usually the ones that were learned in childhood. Look at your parents belief systems to discover them. These may not be messages you agree with today but they are often still operating from your unconscious.) You may or may not feel comfortable disclosing the details of this experience with your partner.

1. What were the accompanying physical and emotional feelings?

2. Was the secret told? Were the beliefs brought to light? What were the results?

3. Tune into the feelings you have and share those with your partner if you can.

Differences in Coming Out

"The personal is political." Some people consider being out to be a very important political statement. Others consider it an issue of personal privacy. Partners can differ in how long they've identified as lesbian (if they use that label), and what it means. Different coming out histories will certainly affect a woman's views and personal choices. A woman who came out at 13 has a good chance of having a significantly different experience from her partner who came out at 32 or at 51.

Partners often find they have circumstantial differences with accompanying pressures, i.e., children, custody issues, employment situations, family and friend networks, and public roles. All these influence decisions about coming out. Again, these differences don't necessarily mean conflict. Problems arise when someone is threatened and judgments are made about one perspective being better than the other.

We've all questioned our appearance at one time or another with regard to coming out. Is this look too obvious? Too femme? Too butch? Too confusing? OK, sometimes the only thing close to comfortable is a sleeping bag — zipped up! Partners often differ in defining what being "out" means. For one person being out means public displays of affection anywhere, anytime and to her partner it means going to the same event at the same time.

When it comes to appearances, how we decorate our home, or if we have separate bedrooms, can also be a coming out issue. How "out" our home looks to family or straight friends can be more important to one partner than the other. "De-dyking" the house or "straightening up" the apartment just prior to visits from family or friends is not just a joke for dyke comics.

Positive regard, respect and acceptance of differences is the most secure foundation for a healthy, viable relationship. If used frequently and liberally, the following exercises are antidotes to homophobic toxicity, and can bridge what may seem like impossibly wide canyons of discord.

Exercise 18 — Inventory   ♀

1. How important is the issue of coming out to you?

Pause & Reflect

2. How important do you think it is to your partner?

3. What methods do you currently use to deal with any differences you have in coming out? (e.g., avoidance of the issue, arguments, blaming, calm discussions, separate social activities, separate family events, etc.)

The next exercise introduces a simple but difficult communication tool useful in resolving differences. It's an exercise in taking turns, thus slowing down the dialogue in order to develop patience, listening abilities and thoughtful speech. This leads to a higher likelihood of resolution. (A more advanced method of "active listening" is described in Chapter 8, *Speaking Up*.)

EXERCISE 19 — *Dealing With Differences: "The Talking Stick"* ♀/♀♀

1. Select a handy item to be your "talking stick" (e.g. a pen, a rock, a shell, a tampon, or even a stick!).

2. Take a few of minutes to identify a problem you experience in your relationship concerning coming out. Ask yourself these questions:
   ▾ How do I feel about this?
   ▾ What do I think about this?
   ▾ What does this mean to me or about me?

3. Taking turns, the speaker holds the talking stick and speaks from her own experience using "I" statements (e.g. "I feel _____ about _____," "I think _____").

4. Express four statements, and then pass the stick to your partner, who then expresses four statements, and trade the stick back again until there is nothing more to be said about this item at this time.

Variations:

A. Each speaker holds the talking stick until she is finished with her thoughts, then passes it. The stick continues back and forth in this manner.

B. Each speaker has a set amount of time with the talking stick before passing it to her partner.

Resources for Dealing with Differences

Books

Books such as this one and others on lesbian and gay issues help give a larger perspective on this issue. Browse at your local booksellers or use the wide reach of the internet.

Counseling

Individual therapy and couples counseling can be an important help in sorting out and resolving emotional barriers and communication problems that interfere with your relationship. Take the time to get references for counselors trained in couples work, ask about their specific experience or feelings working with lesbians, and make sure you both have a reasonable liking of the person you choose.

Friends

Talk to friends about the issue of coming out in their relationships. Share your feelings and ask for support and acceptance of the difficulties you experience. Do this individually and as a couple.

Groups

It is helpful to remember that coming out is an ongoing process. Issues involved in coming out often touch deep fears and are quite challenging. Coming out groups can be helpful at any point. They are not only for those first coming out. They can also be a safe place to deal with the differences you experience on the subject *in* your relationship.

Workshops & Talks

Attendance at workshops and/or talks on coming out, communication, sexuality and other gay issues help raise our consciousness. When they are attended as a couple, workshops and/or talks give you a chance to discuss your differences.

Melody and Dinah

It has taken a lot of work for Mel and Di to learn to refrain from expressing judgments about each other's ways of being out. That is not to say that they do not have judgments, rather it is that they have found it's not productive to include them in discussions. They try their best to acknowledge when they are incapable of such restraint and they take a time out. They're not perfect, though, and they have occasional slips. Their belief in each other's good will has strengthened with the efforts they've been making, enabling them to weather the slips and contain the damage.

They have used the talking stick routine described above with good results. Mel likened it to using training wheels for deep listening. With practice, they are becoming more conscious and skilled communicators. They are usually able to take each situation as it comes and respectfully work out a compromise. By doing so, some standard solutions have emerged.

When they put in an emergency call to a plumber it was decided that whomever was staying home to deal with the plumber got to employ her approach regarding being out. They've employed that solution for all such household emergencies. However, they also have agreed that if one of them must be taken to the hospital for a medical emergency it will be made clear that they are a lesbian couple. When they volunteer together on a political campaign they have agreed to be out to those people they work with consistently, but not to be out to the general public.

Mel now understands that Dinah is not ashamed of her or of their relationship. Dinah realizes some of the benefits of publicly acknowledging their relationship, although her comfort level with being the center of attention does not match Mel's. Both have come to better understand the role homophobia has played in their reactions. Dinah has had to confront her beliefs that being perceived as a lesbian is inherently dangerous and to assess the immediate situation instead of approaching all situations with a single assumption. Mel saw that the importance of receiving her family's acknowledgment related to the limited opportunity the couple had for such acknowledgment in other arenas of their lives. Once some of the charge of their responses lessened, they worked creatively to address both sets of needs. Dinah committed to attending the family gathering after Mel's brother and sister-in-law agreed to have a round of toasts to all couples present, asking those who had been together a year or less to stand, those two years or less and so forth. Everyone loved the idea. Dinah felt assured of not being singled out and Mel and Di were recognized as a couple within the context of all the other partnerships in the family.

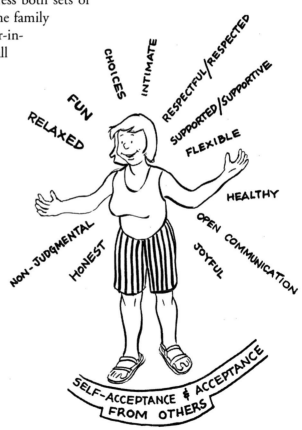

Coming out and being out is a continuing process for Mel and Di, as well as for the rest of us — individually and collectively. Respect and regard for yourself and your partner, good communication, and the reassurance of being cared for goes a long way toward making the process a gentler and mutually supportive one.

Chapter 7

Cycles of Long-Term Relationships

"Life is a process of becoming, a combination of states we have to go through. Where people fail is that they wish to elect a state and remain in it. This is a kind of death."

ANAIS NIN

Stages

No model about relationships fits everyone's experience and none should ever be taken as gospel. The model we offer here is a compilation. It combines our experiences and perspectives and several models presented by others, most notably, D. Merilee Clunis & G. Dorsey Green from *Lesbian Couples,* Seal Press, (2000) and David P. McWhirter & Andrew M. Mattison from *The Male Couple,* Prentis-Hall Trade (1985).

A model helps you recognize where you are and shows paths others have taken before. It's like having a map in the middle of a forest. There are many routes to where you're going that are not always visible from your vantage point. It is comforting to know what is around the bend and to see how to get to your destination.

While this model is presented in a linear fashion, it is not likely to be followed in a linear way. Nor is it necessarily desirable to do so. Relationships are alive and cyclic. One goes through stages again and again in small and in large ways, sometimes completing a cycle in a day or week, sometimes in years. Certain passages resurface throughout the life of the relationship and continue to revolve for the duration of the relationship.

The stages of an adult romantic relationship roughly parallel the stages of the child/parent relationship (see chart at right). Why bring this comparison up you may ask? Because in both situations there exist the powerful issues of bonding, secure attachment, autonomy and individuation. Most of us are somewhat aware of the impact our early relationships with parent figures have on us. A safe and secure childhood attachment is something that informs our emotional, mental and physical health as well as our abilities to create and sustain adult relationships. While our adult relationships recreate some of the same problem issues that existed in our childhood experience they also create an opportunity to heal those issues by more successfully traversing the developmental territory the second time around.

While it may not always feel like it, we do bring some adult qualities to our romantic relationships. The equal responsibility and power inherent in healthy adult partnerships differs significantly from that between parent and child. As adults we have more autonomy and choice than we did as children. We have the capability of entering the relationship as equals, rather than the dependence of child on parent. In primary adult relationships we are inter-dependent. We depend on each other for the well being of the relationship. Each of the preceding stages in this sequence prepares the participants to take on the challenges and tasks of the subsequent stages.

We shortchange ourselves and our relationships of the full experience of each stage if we attempt to jump prematurely to another stage. Such jumps can give us a severe case of emotional whiplash and a precarious foundation to build on. We don't expect a six-month-old to feed the dog, and we shouldn't expect a new relationship to have the comfort and familiarity of an old married couple.

CHILD/PARENT STAGES AND THEIR CORRESPONDING RELATIONSHIP STAGES

CHILD/PARENT STAGES	ADULT ROMANTIC PARTNERSHIP STAGES
1. Parent and infant bonding includes mutual gazing, touch and sound of voice create initial attachment.	1. Courting/Honeymoon: mutual gazing, touch and shared intimacies create initial attachment.
2. Toddler's individuation starts as child begins to assert individual needs, protests conformity.	2. Conflict Stage: power struggles arise, value differences and skill levels become known, protests are made in an attempt to eliminate differences.
3. Parental acceptance of the childs autonomy and personality while continuing to assure secure attachment.	3. Acceptance Stage: lovers accepting each others' autonomy and personal characteristics while reassuring each other of secure connection.
4. Parent and child relationship redefined based on the child's maturation and skill level.	4. Commitment Stage: lovers redefining their relationship based on maturation and skill levels.
5. Parent and child collaborating and building together as the child is able to contribute to mutual projects.	5. Collaborating: building a life together, possibly making a home, children, etc.
6. Parent and child enjoying companionable time free of conflict and strivings.	6. Coasting Stage: couples enjoying companionable time free of conflict and strivings, secure attachment felt.
7. Parent and child maintaining their relationship with shared activities.	7. Renewing Stage: couples consciously find new common interests, fall in love again.
8. Parent and child separating as the child ventures independently into the world.	8. Letting Go: the relationship is redefined, dissolves or one person dies.

Stage 1: Courting/Honeymoon

Courting

The courting stage may exist for a day, a week, or sometimes, for years. It's the stage where you begin to realize that there is an interest in another person, and yes, an attraction. You take the time to make inquiries. You plan activities together. So far it is no different from starting a friendship. While the activities may be the same, the time together will be defined differently. For those interested in romance, it's the start of dating. In all cases, both parties will likely be on their best behavior and "lookin' good."

Honeymoon

The honeymoon is exciting, delicious and a bit nerve-wracking. This stage may take place anywhere from a week or a month to two years into a relationship. In this "state of mind" there is a delightful mutual delusion about the relationship and each other based on needs and projections. She is "all I could hope for" in a partner (unlike my past mistakes). There is passion and intensity. In the process of falling in love, or falling in lust, there is a sense of oneness, or merging. "I can't tell where she begins and I leave off, we have so much in common!" Differences or conflicts are minimized or denied. For example, in this stage you don't mention that you can't stand her best friend. You believe she'll come to view things your way in time because she's reasonable and certainly wouldn't want you to be uncomfortable.

While this stage has its wonderful points, it is common to mistakenly equate this phase with a "good" relationship, believing that this euphoria will last forever. From love songs to soap operas, this misconception is reinforced by the media. When this stage is over, many women discard the relationship, and in doing so, perhaps pass up an incredible find.

A common pitfall for lesbians is to leap from the honeymoon to stage five, collaborating. Activities such as moving in or buying a house together, sharing all funds or getting a dog are often too quickly undertaken. Such a premature bid for security makes the inevitable conflict stage more risky. There are high stakes involved.

Tasks

The tasks of the Courting/Honeymoon stage are:

- ▼ to find and connect with someone you're "attracted" to and discover all you have in common
- ▼ to form an attachment and bond
- ▼ to have fun and companionship
- ▼ to create positive projections and fantasies of "what could be" to sufficiently carry you through the conflict stage

Barriers

The barriers to reaching this stage are:

- ▼ lack of available partners due to lesbian invisibility or low population
- ▼ lack of common meeting places
- ▼ extreme shyness or lack of self-esteem
- ▼ being unacceptable by cultural standards of appearance
- ▼ the potential danger of showing affection in public places
- ▼ racism
- ▼ ageism
- ▼ classism
- ▼ internalized homophobia

 Pause & Reflect

Skills

The skills necessary for this stage are:

- ▼ basic communication and social ability
- ▼ the ability to initiate and respond
- ▼ enough self-esteem to present oneself in a positive light

EXERCISE 20 — *Fantasy Date* ♀

Plan a fantasy date with someone new. Imagine how you ask for the date, and what you do on the date. What information would you like from her? What do you want to let her know?

EXERCISE 21 — *What is Romance?* ♀/♑

1. Ask yourself what constitutes a romantic experience for you.

2. Do you know what constitutes a romantic experience for your partner/date?

3. Share some of this with her.

Stage 2: Conflict

Yes, Harriet, conflict abounds. As naturally as night follows day, the moon follows the sun, and rivers flow into the sea conflict enters into every relationship where there is honesty and intimacy. This is not bad. There are inevitable differences in every human relationship, mis-assumptions and unmet expectations, disappointments and spats. This is not bad either. We can only be on our "best behavior" for so long and then the bigger picture begins to emerge. Our values and tastes become apparent, we have swings of highs and lows, "patterns" start to show and the legacies of negative family training surface. This does not make us bad. This is a stage of both harmony and dissonance. (For some it may be the beginning of attempts to "remake" the other person into their ideal. This is not good.) The conflict stage is very important and one filled with tasks that, if successfully achieved, will serve the relationship well for its duration. This stage need not signify the beginning of the end, but it does signify the end of the beginning.

Example: In this stage you let her know you don't like her best friend and you don't understand what she sees in her. You finally tell her you don't want "her" coming to the house. Feelings are hurt, defenses go up and discussions follow.

Tasks

The tasks of the Conflict stage include:

- first and foremost, learning how to deal with differences in ways that don't threaten the security of the relationship
- expressing anger in a non-abusive fashion
- being assertive and negotiating
- tolerating many of the differences
- learning that your happiness does not depend on her moods
- creating rules and boundaries
- reassuring her that you deeply care
- identifying resources and deciding how they get used

As resources are identified, (physical or emotional abilities, spiritual perspectives, time and attention, money and skills) there can be conflict over mis-matched abilities, or how to best use the resources in the relationship. This is an opportunity to negotiate, to learn balance and trust. Trust is learned when one's actions consistently match one's words over a period of time, and when good intentions are communicated despite mistakes.

Dealing with differences and muddling through conflicts can help identify assumed beliefs, deepest fears, and worst defenses. It starts the process of creating mutual rules and boundaries. This is important to establishing security and togetherness, autonomy and interdependence.

Barriers

OK, take a deep breath, this is a big list. The barriers to getting through this stage intact consist of two categories. The first is past wounds and fears; the second is current mistaken or conflicting beliefs and values.

In the first category are:

- fears of conflict
- low self-esteem
- insecurity
- mistrust in one's own skills
- lack of successful models
- lack of communication skills
- past abuse (emotional, physical, sexual)
- dysfunctional family histories
- passivity or aggressiveness
- internalized homophobia
- Defensiveness and/or dishonesty
- all addictions or co-dependent behaviors

Hold on, there's more... in the second category, are:

- beliefs and assumptions about race, class, religion, size and age that are confining or prejudicial
- unhealthy beliefs and assumptions about relationships

For example, equating compromise with giving up your self, or dependence with giving up your self, are hindering beliefs. Equating love with the other knowing all your needs is just as problematic. (More on these later.)

Skills

The skills needed for completion of the Conflict stage are:

- communication — the ability to listen with compassion and reveal one's vulnerabilities
- development of effective negotiation patterns and problem-solving

- boundary setting and boundary flexibility — the ability to say "no" and the ability to say "yes" based on one's true needs and preferences

- the ability to make compromises and to consider your partner's needs as important

- impulse control: the ability to take turns, put your feelings on temporary hold, make considered decisions, delay immediate gratification, etc.

- tolerance of being misunderstood

- tolerance of feelings (one's own and one's partner's)

- the ability to maintain a view of the "larger picture," a larger or long-term perspective

- a sense of individuality and autonomy ("I am ok on my own")

- self-love

- willingness and desire to work through difficulties

- tolerance of non-abusive conflict

- intolerance of abuse

- tolerance of another's emotions without having to "fix" the other person and make her feel differently

- generosity with time and energy

- honesty

- the willingness and ability to look at ourselves and our shortcomings

- the ability to speak one's truth in a non-blaming way

Exercise 22 — List Comparison ♀/♀♀

Note: If you even think you're in this stage, read Chapters 8 & 9, *Speaking Up* and *Fighting Fair*. This exercise is about gaining helpful information, not judging or competing. Try staying focused on what is present, not what is lacking.

1. Review the skills list and rate your skill level. Use a scale of 0 to 10: 0 being not at all and 10 being in abundance.

2. Compare your list with your partner's. If you'd like to expound on your own skills (or lack of) do so, but don't comment on her list. This is about developing awareness and noticing where your perceptions differ.

Exercise 23 — Positive Choices   ♀

1. Take a long look at the skills you feel you don't possess.

2. What do you feel would be helpful in developing or improving one or two of them?

3. Ask for ideas from friends to help with this goal.

4. Put notes up on your mirror; write reminders in your calendar; begin to practice using new skills with your friends and acquaintances. Here, the stakes might not be as high and it could be easier to risk trying new behaviors.

Stage 3: Acceptance

What Is Acceptance?

Partners experiencing successful resolution of conflicts through understanding, empathy, negotiation and mutual problem-solving come to realize that differences don't end the relationship. Each person accepts that she and her beloved are different people — sometimes unimaginably different. Productive relationship patterns create a secure sense of attachment and differences become less problematic. There can even be an appreciation of them.

This stage is characterized by more harmony than dissonance. Optimism about the future returns. Falling in love again and those "honeymoon" feelings from the courting stage can resurge. It's spring in the park again! This time the two of you are familiar with the paths and each have your favorite walks and views. By this stage you can look at your feelings regarding her best friend (for example) and realize how you feel threatened. You can claim your own feelings and the perspectives on which they are based. You can acknowledge her right to have friends and your right to feel secure regarding your place in the relationship. Together you are able to identify what you need for reassurance in the relationship and acknowledge her separate needs for independent connections with others.

Tasks

The tasks of the Acceptance stage are:

- ▼ to accept differences — partners need to stretch their perspectives and see acceptance of differences as a plus in the relationship rather than a minus
- ▼ to regain a sense of the possibilities for the relationship
- ▼ to improve methods of resolving differences in power, preferences and problem solving
- ▼ to each acknowledge her contributions and responsibility in the conflicts and difficulties
- ▼ to each acknowledge her own and her partner's history and patterns
- ▼ to see the other as separate yet intimately connected
- ▼ and last but not least, to continue to reassure each other of their value and importance

Barriers

Barriers to successfully completing this stage include:

- ▼ internalized homophobia
- ▼ defenses against intimacy
- ▼ defenses against abandonment
- ▼ fear of being consumed, disappearing, losing oneself
- ▼ the false assumption that conflict and/or struggle are necessary all of the time

Skills

The skills and resources needed to meet these tasks are:

- ▼ positive self-esteem
- ▼ security with self

- ▼ appreciation and acknowledgment of the other as separate
- ▼ tolerance of happiness (some people are more familiar and comfortable with striving or struggling)
- ▼ openness to change and growth in self and in the relationship
- ▼ development of some common interests and values
- ▼ communication all of the above

The stages of conflict and acceptance (like the other stages) pop up all through our relationships — again and again. The first round is often the most threatening. Successfully navigating these initial stages assures each person that they, and their relationship, can survive and actually thrive.

Exercise 24 — Culinary Adventures ♀/♀

1. Identify an area where you and your beloved are clearly different (spicy and sweet).

2. List in your mind or on paper the dilemmas this presented in the past (indigestion?).

3. Identify the current challenges this difference presents.

4. List the benefits you and your relationship have due to this difference (a varied diet).

5. List the characteristics each of you has developed in order to accept these differences and benefits.

6. Compare your lists with each other.

EXERCISE 25 — *Celebrating Differences*   ♀

---

1. Jot down some of the ways you criticize your partner for being different from you.

2. Write how you would feel receiving such messages.

3. What benefits do you derive from these differences? Take your time. There are some (often hidden) benefits to almost every difference.

4. How can you communicate these benefits to your partner?

Stage 4: Commitment

In this stage, one or both individuals begins to feel a stronger, more longstanding commitment to the relationship. Perhaps they feel the need for a mutually understood definition of commitment. We're talking monogamy vs. non-monogamy, rings and things, spending every weekend together.

Perhaps this is a time when you decide there is a need for mutual friends and the desire to do more as a couple. You may wish to have a public ceremony to declare your intentions. You may exchange rings privately. It is a time when couples draw up wills that protect each other or get durable power of attorney for health care. Falling in love again can be an outcome of successful maneuvering through the gates of The Big "C."

Tasks

The tasks of the Commitment stage are to define what is a comfortable commitment and to determine "liberating structures" for the relationship. Liberating structures are agreements or behaviors that help give each person a sense of security, a sense of boundaries, and rules that are clear yet have some flexibility. These structures are many and range from no touching during a fight to cuddling every other night from 9:30–10:00, to monthly housemeetings on finances and chores, to separate households. The possibilities are endless. A "liberating" structure promotes well-being in the individuals and in the relationship. It does not seek to restrict and control.

Defining a commitment goes hand in hand with finding liberating structures. While some of this "defining" is likely to have occured earlier in the relationship, the likelihood of a common or realistic commitment is slim before the conflict and acceptance stages are reached. Earlier commitments are usually based on projection, fantasy, insecurity or fear.

Barriers

Barriers to this process include:

- differing values
- differing life goals
- incomplete resolution of the conflict or acceptance stages
- lack of role models and support
- lack of rituals and recognition
- lack of benefits
- lack of validation from family, culture and friends
- fears of feeling trapped

Skills

The skills necessary for completion of this stage are:

- trust in oneself and the other person
- self-knowledge
- valuing collaboration
- communication and assertiveness

▼ recognizing the difference between healthy interdependent commitment and co-dependent commitment. (Co-dependent commitment is characterized by rescuing, controlling and placating the other person rather than a commitment to helping each other grow.)

EXERCISE 26 — Freewriting ♀

1. Write the word "commitment" at the top of a page.

2. Put a pen or pencil in your non-dominant hand. (The one you don't usually write with.)

3. Close your eyes and take a deep breath.

4. Open your eyes and start writing whatever comes into your head. This is free association; it doesn't need to make sense.

5. Keep writing for 10 minutes, without pausing to think or rest. If you get stuck, simply write "I'm stuck," or "Blah, blah, blah," until the next thought pops up. This is called freewriting.

6. Turn your pages over when you're done, take a break, and then come back to them. Read what you've written and notice all the associations you have with commitment. This can tell you something important about why you relate to the commitment stage the way you do.

EXERCISE 27 — What is Commitment? ♀/♀♀

Definitions of commitment include sharing responsibilities, sharing possessions, how decisions are made, how much time is spent together, fidelity and ways of being taken care of.

1. What are tangible signs of commitment for you?

Pause & Reflect

2. How do you imagine your partner would answer number one?

3. Share this information with your partner.

Stage 5: Collaborating

In this stage there are many tasks that require collaboration and joint effort. These are not usually possible without pooled energies and resources. Experience with successful problem-solving and productive patterns of relating are necessary to take on the tasks of this stage. Such successes indicate that the relationship has sufficient strength and structural integrity to bear the weight and pressure these endeavors inevitably bring. It is helpful to remember that these stages are cyclic — relationships go in and out of this stage with small and large undertakings continuing through the life of the relationship (from planning a weekend away to buying a house).

Here are more examples from this stage:

- jointly selecting a birthday present
- assembling furniture together
- working on a community or organizational project
- saving money towards a mutual goal, such as travel

- purchasing items together
- co-parenting children
- sharing a pet (co-petting)
- planting a garden
- arranging for shared insurance or other plans for security in the future
- collaborating in the care of family members
- completing power of attorney for health care naming each other as the responsible party

Tasks

The tasks of the Collaboration stage include the following:

- dreaming together
- mutually designing the big picture of what is wanted
- identifying and choreographing the necessary steps
- agreeing on the resources needed and arranging for them
- clarifying roles and division of labor
- keeping on through disappointments and trying times.
- avoiding blaming each other for the disappointments and trying times
- negotiating conflicts
- establishing dependability

Barriers

This stage has certain potential barriers.

- the high stakes involved can result in increased anxiety, desire for control and subsequent conflicts
- boundaries can be forgotten and issues of trust arise if the pursuit of the goal overshadows the value of being partners
- old defensive behaviors can reappear — partners can assume they've seriously regressed and give up in despair
- lack of negotiation and/or assertion skills can lead to confusion and decisions of default instead of consideration
- lack of confidence can mean acquiesce instead of collaborating
- health concerns mean one partner may not have the energy or ability to collaborate equally
- addictions will compromise all decision making processes
- depression or other mood disorders will also impair communication and collaboration skills
- one or the other partner basically mistrusts the other's skills or character
- grandiose, unrealistic goals result in more pressure than the relationship can bear

Skills

Skills, skills, skills. Yes, there are skills that make it possible to successfully wind your way through this stage. They are:

- ▾ realistic planning that takes shared values, goals and resources into consideration
- ▾ problem-solving
- ▾ negotiating
- ▾ valuing follow-through on commitments
- ▾ trusting and being trustworthy (when deeds match words over a period of time)
- ▾ being honest in non-blaming ways
- ▾ tolerating deferred gratification
- ▾ valuing the health and well-being of the individuals first, then the relationship, then the project

EXERCISE 28 — Hi Ho, Hi Ho...It's Off to Work We Go   ♀/♀♀

With your partner, select a mutually desired project that you both wish to complete in the near future. Select a simple and easy one the first time you do this exercise and then return to a bigger, more elaborate one. Now complete questions one through eight by yourself.

1. List all the reasons you find this project desirable.

2. List all the reasons you wish to collaborate with your partner on this project.

3. Identify whatever barriers you may foresee.

4. Identify the resources, i.e., time, raw materials, space, tools, equipment, additional people, money, you and your partner have readily available for this endeavor.

5. Identify the skills and talents you and your partner have and will use.

6. Describe the resources you will need to obtain.

7. Describe the relational skills you need to successfully complete this quest, such as, "I need to speak up when I've reached my physical limits instead of shutting down and becoming resentful."

8. List the relational skills you want demonstrated, such as "I want us to be clear on when we will complete our parts."

9. Compare your answers and discuss your results with each other.

Stage 6: Coasting

In the coasting stage, partners sit back and appreciate what they've built so far in the relationship. This stage or part of the cycle comes at a time when trust and safety are established. There is a shift in attitude which is sometimes felt as a sense of relief. This shift includes a feeling of security, and sometimes a sense of routine. This is a time of respite from struggle, when the relationship seems to run smoothly all on its own. (Thank goodness!)

Tasks

The tasks of the Coasting stage are:

- ▾ to enjoy life

- ▾ to appreciate the feelings of security and contentment

- ▾ to let go of power struggles

- ▾ to be aware that not all problems need to be solved today

- ▾ To actively appreciate each other (say it out loud, show it in actions!)

Barriers

There are barriers to this stage, and some of them may seem a bit strange. One barrier is the inability to tolerate happiness and serenity. This can come from low self-esteem ("I don't deserve to feel this good") or lack of familiarity ("This feels very different, something must be wrong"). These feelings most often stem from chaotic family history or experiences that have had a negative impact on self-worth. Another barrier to this more peaceful stage is a discomfort with routine or sameness. This can be felt as boredom. A common reaction is for one or both partners to do something negative to stir things up. A productive response is to think creatively about infusing the relationship (or the individual who is bored) with some interesting experiences.

Another frequent consequence of this stage and its serenity is for each partner to take the other for granted. It can be a time of complacency or a time when one person feels trapped. Sometimes this is experienced as the famous "seven-year itch," which, sorry to say, lesbians are not immune to.

For example, you find yourself coming home from work day after day. "Hi, honey I'm home." You feed the animals, fix something to eat and the two of you watch TV for the evening's entertainment. You are only vaguely interested in hearing about her day at work (it's just the same old stuff) and you don't feel any urgent need to tell her about the argument you had with your friend. By now you've heard so much about each other's lives that each day does not feel like a beginning. Life is fine, but not too exciting.

This scenario may be heaven on earth to some of you, but to others, it sounds like life in a coma. The latter woman might begin to have a roving eye, have a crisis at work, fall off the wagon or some other such dramatic infusion to shake things up. But this is not the only way to bring in interest and excitement, and less destructive choices are preferable. The skills listed below can help you smoothly sail through the more disruptive impulses that can occur during the coasting stage.

Skills

- ▾ continued communication about feelings, ideas, events

- ▾ patience

- ▾ creativity to infuse new ideas, people, fun and goals into the relationship

- ▾ consistency

- ▾ understanding

- ▾ renewed commitment to making one's own life healthy and challenging

- ▾ willingness to bring to the relationship, not just get from it

EXERCISE 29 — Appreciations   ⚲/⚲⚲

1. Come up with one thing you can do each and every day to let your partner know she is appreciated.

pause & Reflect

2. Do it.

EXERCISE 30 — New Juice   ♀

1. Think of something you've always thought was exciting, interesting or challenging to do but that you never got around to doing — a personal goal.

2. Outline plans to do it.

3. If you get stuck because of lack of resources or time, go back to step one of this exercise and think of something else. Continue until you have one "do-able" goal for infusing your life with a little new juice.

Stage 7: Renewing

The renewing stage is characterized by a resurgence of falling in love and the enjoyment of the deep satisfactions a secure relationship brings. At this point you both share a common history. You draw on that history to know that while conflicts still occur, they are resolvable and containable. Differences are present (even enjoyed), acknowledged, negotiated and accepted — sooner or later. It is possible to remember that difficult times pass and do not last forever. It is now evident that the relationship doesn't "do itself" for long periods of time. It requires quality time and attention.

Tasks

The tasks of the Renewing stage include:

- shifting from self-centeredness to flexible awareness of self, your partner and the relationship

- recommitting to the lighter side of relationship, to play and sharing

- maintaining a larger perspective (i.e. the cosmic picture "I am not the center of the universe," "things do pass and overall we do pretty well")

- consciously reserving quality time and energy for the relationship (special evenings and outings, celebrating anniversaries, taking time away for just the two of you, keeping current with each other, expressing loving feelings in actions and words)

- acknowledging the partnership in various realms (work, family, friends and community)

- being creative in keeping the romance alive (notes, surprises, kisses)

Barriers

Barriers in this stage are often external to the relationship. However, they can be factors in the lives of the individual partners and, consequently, have significant impact on the relationship:

- individual life tasks (career issues, children and parenting concerns, midlife or later changes, retirement)

- health concerns

- addictions

- depression and other mood disorders

- extended family responsibilities such as aging parents, nieces and nephews, close friends, siblings

Skills

Continue to develop these internal abilities and outward expressions:

- ▾ valuing oneself and one's partner
- ▾ committing quality energy and attention to the relationship
- ▾ further accepting of differences
- ▾ Having personal flexibility
- ▾ expressing passion, affection and renewed appreciation
- ▾ valuing play and humor
- ▾ continuing to resolve internalized homophobia
- ▾ identifying to others that you are in this partnership
- ▾ taking responsibility for self-care

Exercise 31 — The "Surprise" Date   ♀♀

1. Gather your calendars and reserve at least two days, evenings, or weekends in the next month for the two of you. (You might choose one evening per week, or a day every other weekend, or one weekend a month — whatever schedule fits for you.) Be specific and realistic.

2. Discuss general concerns such as cost, distance, food, place or recreation preferences.

3. Each take responsibility for one of your "surprise dates." The responsible person is to choose and plan the activity, make whatever arrangements are necessary, and to keep it a secret.

4. The "datee" is to let go and enjoy herself to the best of her ability. She can pass on any activity she feels uncomfortable with, of course. If this happens, you can negotiate a version you would mutually enjoy.

Stage 8: Letting Go

The only constant in life and in relationships is change. If the transformations are gradual and fit with our expectations, we often don't take note of them. Yet conscious or not, dramatic or not, welcomed or not, our relationships go through a process of constant adjustment.

With every change, there is some loss and some gain. The losses are often the most intensely felt part of transformation. It is common to go through some form of denial, bargaining, anger, sadness, and eventually acceptance to reach resolution on the larger changes.

Let's take a look at these steps that lead to resolution. Denial is the psyche's automatic defense mechanism against the pain of loss. It is the tendency to disbelieve that anything is "wrong" in the relationship or the inability to grasp the magnitude of a change that has taken place. Bargaining is the tendency to try and make a deal with yourself, with the other person or with a greater power to bring things back to the way they were. Lots of retrospective bargaining goes on too ("If only I had..."). Anger is usually a part of dealing with change and loss. There can be anger for the adjustments one needs to make, blame for the other person for the feelings that arise or the changes that have occurred (even if the person is no longer there to blame). Sadness can range from deeply depressing, "Life is too painful to manage" thoughts to mild twinges of melancholy. Acceptance of change comes in bits and pieces. It includes a certain sense of resolution about the changes that have taken place, a sense of having made some peace with them.

Grief

Each of these feelings regarding change and loss will come and go, and not necessarily in this sequence. The feelings come in cycles, and the cycles usually spin several times.

"Letting go" is an important stage that accompanies all evolution in our relationships including the inevitable conclusion, which is that all relationships will eventually come to an end (at least on the physical plane). "Letting go" also applies to the sundry, everyday assortment of losses, gains and adjustments that we encounter in our relationships, as well as dramatic life-changing ones that come from being mortal and loving other mortal beings. These include physical or emotional disability, illness, separation, break-up and death. Appropriately, much has been written on illness, death, grief and loss. We're not attempting to fully address these topics here. However, the following lists of tasks, barriers and skills will be helpful and apply to any level of loss or change. Some of these tasks might be accomplished in a matter of hours, or they might take years, depending on the magnitude of the change or loss. There is no right way or proper schedule for moving through these tasks.

Tasks

The tasks of the Letting Go stage are:

- being aware that changes, losses and transformations occur in all relationships
- acknowledging these changes, their effects and the feelings you and your partner have about them
- accepting that bargaining with yourself, others, God, Goddess, Great Spirit or the universe about these changes is a natural part of this process
- being aware of your irritation, anger, and even rage, and expressing them in healthy ways
- acknowledging your sadness and expressing that in healthy ways
- accepting the feelings you have about these changes even if you don't accept the changes
- seeking and accepting support from others to help weather the changes
- expressing your feelings in a non-blaming way to your partner or being honest about being unable to do so
- doing your best to accept the feelings your partner has or being honest about it when you cannot accept or listen to her feelings
- releasing your relationship's previous form to what is next
- if necessary and when possible, forgiving and releasing your partner or the previous state of your relationship
- accepting the changes, losses and gains these transformations have brought you
- providing loving self-care in response to your needs and preferences

Barriers

The barriers of this stage are simultaneously familiar and new:

- unresolved previous losses and grief
- unrelenting denial of change and losses
- compulsive need to prevent or control changes and/or losses
- intolerance of unpleasant feelings in self and/or others
- negative judgment and rejection of one's own and/or the others' feelings

- inability to express feelings to others

- lack of boundaries, resulting in the others' feelings being heard as information about oneself instead of information about others

- isolation from others physically and/or emotionally

- numbing and avoiding feelings through compulsive activities (work, socializing, sex, caretaking others, drugs and alcohol)

- attaching to one phase of grief and fearing moving on (denial, bargaining, anger, sadness/depression)

- venting anger in hostile or abusive ways

- unrealistic expectations of oneself or one's partner to "get on with life" before resolution with the changes has been reached

- failing to develop or use personal or outside resources

- shame, self-criticism and self-blame

- blaming others without looking at one's own role

- engaging in self-destructive behaviors

- Seeking to gain power through intimidation or unkindness to others

Skills

Most of the skills necessary for successful completion of the Letting Go stage will have been practiced and honed in previous stages of relationship. Now it's time to cash in on your hard-won experience and wisdom. If they weren't developed then, you guessed it — you'll get the opportunity now!

Though these are not strictly "skills, they are choices you can make that help with letting go:

- being honest and caring with yourself and your partner about the changes and whatever feelings accompany them

- tolerating one's own and others' intense and unpleasant feelings

- ▼ remembering that others' feelings are information about them and their experience — it is not information about you

- ▼ having compassion for yourself and others

- ▼ talking to safe, supportive people about your experiences and feelings

- ▼ allowing the time and space necessary for each of you to work your way through the stages of denial, bargaining, anger, sadness and acceptance

- ▼ utilizing your personal resources during this time (writing, reflection, meditation, prayer, art, music, ritual, readings, self-care routines)

- ▼ utilizing outside sources of support (family, friends, therapists, spiritual advisors/teachers, support groups, classes on grieving/loss)

- ▼ seeking a balance of solitude, activities and interaction with others

- ▼ keeping life as simple as possible, avoiding unnecessary tasks and complications

- ▼ refraining from making big decisions, instead, take your time to let all of the factors settle in

- ▼ being especially gentle and nurturing to yourself

- ▼ allowing yourself extra time to do things

- ▼ consciously being aware of staying safe while driving, walking, traveling

- ▼ doing those things that especially bring you satisfaction and comfort

- ▼ refraining from overuse of alcohol, drugs, sex, food, shopping and other compulsive activities

- ▼ trusting that feelings do pass and that wounds can heal

- ▼ being kind to each other and yourself to the best of your abilities

EXERCISE 32 — Pillow Talk   ♀

If you find yourself being overwhelmed with feelings or unable to access under-the-surface feelings, a little "pillow work" may be in order. Do this on a comfortable surface such as carpeting or a bed, and use a good, thick pillow. This exercise is intended to help you access and release constricted or painful feelings so you can have relief and clarity. Switching roles can bring insight and understanding.

1. Give yourself enough time, space and solitude to feel comfortable and without the worry of interruption. If you're uncomfortable doing this exercise outloud, try writing it down as a spontaneous dialogue.

2. Sitting on the floor or on a bed, position a solid pillow in front of you.

3. Imagine that your partner or a part of the change that you may have feelings about is sitting on the pillow (e.g., a new schedule, financial difficulties, illness). Take a big breath and tune in to how you feel about that person or that part.

4. Allow yourself to say whatever comes to mind to this imaginary audience.

5. Continue talking until there is nothing else to say.

6. Breathe and tune in again. Continue if there is anything else.  *Pause & Reflect*

7. Take a break.

8. Now imagine that you are your partner or the part of the change that you were addressing.

9. Imagine yourself sitting on the pillow across from you. Again, allow yourself to say whatever comes to mind (speak as your partner or that part of the change).

10. Continue until there is nothing else to say. Breathe, and tune in to how you feel.

Exercise 33 — Pillow Pounding: Anger Release 1   ♀

This exercise is designed to help you to get in touch with and release anger. (Note: Do not do this exercise if you have or are recovering from any upper body or back injury!)

1. Give yourself enough time, space and solitude to feel comfortable and without the worry of interruption.

2. Sitting on the floor or on a bed, position a solid pillow in front of you.

3. If there are any angry feelings (from irritation or resentment to rage), notice how and where in your body you experience these. If you're not in touch with any anger, proceed anyway.

4. Clasp your hands together in front of you.

5. With arms extended, raise your hands to eye level or higher and then bring them down on the pillow. Exhale as you hit the pillow.

6. Hit the pillow five times, breathe, and relax your shoulders.

7. Hit the pillow five more times. Let yourself vocalize whatever words or sounds come to your mind.

8. Continue hitting the pillow in sets of five until there are no more words or feelings.

9. Breathe, relax and tune in to how you are feeling.

10. Give yourself time to rest, write, draw, talk to a friend, or go for a walk.

EXERCISE 34 — Temper Tantrum: Anger Release 2

This is yet another way to release anger, discover underlying feelings and gain clarity. It's for those times when structure and self-control are less desired or less available. Flailing about in full voice can be quite satisfying.

1. Find an empty bedroom.

2. Lie on the bed (face down or face up).

3. Kick, pound, writhe and flail away!

4. Scream or yell to your hearts content (often screaming into a pillow is less scary to do and less alarming for others).

5. Continue until you're finished (you're the judge of what's enough).

6. Breathe, relax and tune into how you are feeling.

7. Give yourself time to rest, write, draw, talk to a friend, or go for a walk.

Exercise 35 — Forgiveness and Releasing ♀

Writing letters you never send is a very useful way to get clarity on how you feel about someone and/or a situation. If you are struggling with unclear feelings about changes in your relationship and/or your partner, we invite you to write a letter. Letter writing can be used in this way at any time to deal with any feelings. This particular application is for when you feel ready to forgive or release a partner who isn't present or is in some way unavailable to receive your message. *Do not rush this.* Honestly assess whether you feel forgiving. You may feel forgiving about some things and not others. You can always attend to the parts you can release now and come back and do the others when you are ready. Accept where you are without judgment. Self-criticism does not assist healing.

1. Allow yourself enough time and space to tune in to what you feel about your partner.

2. With pen and paper, list any ways that you have been holding onto her and/or the relationship that you are now ready to release. In this letter let her know that you now release both of you from these holds.

3. In this letter let her know that you now forgive her of any intentional and unintentional harm she may have caused you.

4. In this letter ask her forgiveness of any intentional and unintentional harm you may have caused her.

5. In this letter let her know that you release her to her highest good.

6. Dispose of this letter in the way that suits you. (One favorite is burning it and scattering the ashes in a place or body of water that is special.)

Note: If your partner is accessible, you may choose to give or read this letter to her depending on your current state of communication and your state of mind. Do this only if it feels kind to do so and if you can do so without needing a response. However this exercise is highly effective without involving another.

> *"Holding on to anger is like*
> *grasping a hot coal with the intent of*
> *throwing it at someone else;*
> *you are the one who gets burned."*
> THE BUDDHA

EXERCISE 36 — Transforming Ties That Bind ♀

You can do this exercise alone, have a friend guide you through it, or read the instructions into a tape recorder slowly and play it for yourself. Sometimes this exercise brings up strong emotions. Simply observe what happens to you and let the feelings flow through you without clinging to them.

1. Find a quiet place to lie or sit comfortably. Take the phone off the hook, put out the dog, etc.

2. Close your eyes and take six deep, slow breaths, relaxing your body as you exhale, beginning to quiet your mind and put away the day's tasks or anxieties.

3. With your mind's eye, imagine yourself standing facing the one you are feeling bound to. Imagine that you can see cords of energy or light connecting the two of you. Notice how thick these cords are. Where do they connect the two of you? What are the qualities of these cords — color, texture, feeling?   *Pause & Reflect*

4. Let your intuition be the guide, and make some kind of change in the cord connections. This might mean stretching them, untangling them or cutting all or some of them. There are many creative possibilities here. Find one that works for you.

5. Continue to make changes in the cords until you are finished for now. You can do this exercise many times as you transform your relationships and work toward healing and letting go.

Each of the previous exercises is designed to help you through the inevitable feelings that arise from facing changes and loss in a relationship. It is most helpful to take time with each item on the "Skills" and "Barriers" lists and evaluate your strengths and problem areas. Next, make concrete plans and commitments to develop your skills and work through your own barriers. Letting go is a difficult thing for most of us to do, whether it is letting go of the way you like the furniture arranged, letting go of a job, a particular lifestyle, a relationship, or a life.

The intensity of the grief that comes with loss depends on the strength of the attachment to and involvement with the thing or person that's lost. Grief's path is also influenced by one's previous experiences of loss and trauma, the suddenness of the loss and the personal supports (or lack thereof) in one's life.

Just as the only constant is change, our constant task is to remain present. This determines whether our ultimate experience is one of being enriched and affirmed or impoverished and denied. However modest or far-reaching the effects of change are in our lives, the task of staying emotionally and mentally present remain.

Rhythm

It is wonderful to get a sense of your own rhythm as a couple: sharing initial excitement and newness; struggling and working with differences and conflicts; appreciating each other in deeper ways; acknowledging your partnership; feeling your competencies as a team and seeing the results of your work together; enjoying the familiarity and comfort of "the two of you"; and letting go of the familiar as life's changes continue.

The stages of relationship development presented here are fluid cycles in life. As you compare your complex selves to this simplified model, some stages will likely fit you to a tee; others will need adjustments. As problematic issues resurface, your perspective and ability to negotiate them will change, and likely improve. You can only truly experience where you are.

Your passage through these stages can happen with or without your being aware of it. However, your awareness of this material can facilitate your passage and heighten your experience. Consciousness is a precious thing. With it comes the ability to see from several vantage points, opening the possibility of choices otherwise unknown.

Despite the extra barriers for lesbians, solid, healthy relationships are possible and plentiful. This model can serve as a reference point for discussion and encouragement to all of you who are seeking, and building, satisfying long-term relationships with friends and lovers.

There is an ancient Zen saying: "You can't push the river." Be patient. The river will carry you. You can enjoy the vistas and negotiate the rapids as you go.

Chapter 8

Speaking Up: Raising Your Level of Communication

"Carve not upon a stone when I am dead
The praise which remorseful mourners give
To women's graves — a tardy recompense —
But speak them while I live."
ELIZABETH AKERS ALLEN

Why Focus on Communication?

Relationships are partnerships. We expect to use communication in any mutual endeavor including business, recreation or creative collaboration. You wouldn't expect your business to run smoothly without information exchanged among the boss, employees, customers and even competitors. Rules work better when they are clear. Assumptions and expectations must be made known. Even you and your dog must communicate in order to go on a walk.

But communication in and of itself is not enough. Communication can be used for showing care, respect and reassurance. It can be used for play and pleasure. Or it can be used for destruction, promoting fear or control of others. The communication focused on in this chapter is all intended to enhance the former and reduce the latter.

Many of the messages we give are non-verbal — body language, facial expressions — and many are through tone of voice. The words themselves are communicating only a small portion of what's being said and it behooves us to become aware of the total message we are giving. Keeping a positive intent helps make communication successful.

Healthy partnerships require secure, loving attachment. This goal is enhanced with clear, direct and open communication. Partnerships also require appropriate restraint and conscious kind-

ness. Not all of us have the same idea of what good communication is. Some know what it is but don't have the needed self-control to use it, and others don't even have a clue.

Our perceptions and values are as varied as our pasts and experiences. We each "see" the world through our individual filter. Communication is a necessary bridge, giving us entry to another's inner world and inviting others to share ours. When differences between people are significant, this bridge is essential.

There is a direct correlation between healthy, successful relationships and relationships with a secure sense of connection and consistent openness and communication. (Not all of that communication need be verbal). Along with the ability to differentiate and self-soothe when emotions run high, these relationships are less stressful, more productive and much more fun.

Practicing the skills in this chapter will give you ways to get your message across, increase the chances of getting your needs met, and maintaining your relationship. Some ways of communicating are more productive than others. Communication skills are essential building blocks for all relationships. These skills are learnable, pragmatic, can be used over and over, and can make life easier.

Even with the most brilliant communicators there is no guarantee against snafus and breakdowns. Relational skills are particularly indispensable to lesbians because we have fewer of the built-in advantages, the supportive and cementing structures, or modeling that can help maintain heterosexual relationships.

There are a number of approaches to integrating new methods of communication. Let's use a life jacket as an example. Before using a life jacket it can be instructive to pick it up, examine it, look at the fasteners and construction, and eventually try it on. That's the gradual way of learning and using a new tool. Another way to learn about life jackets is to be forced to use one while the boat is sinking. Ideally, you are already wearing your life jacket. If you are not, there is tremendous incentive to don it quickly and apply all of your attention to fastening it. Although the incentive to wear it is high, the life jacket is harder to use when you are unfamiliar with it. Similarly, practicing the skills in this chapter before you're in "relational deep water" will improve your chances of negotiating conflicts, but grabbing the workbook to use an exercise during a conflict is also helpful (as long as you both are willing.)

Assumptions

If communication is the miracle cure of the century then why don't we all "just do it?" The first reason we don't use this "miracle cure" is because we assume we know what others are thinking and feeling. We then base our expectations and behavior on these wild imaginings. The second is that we instantly react internally, often unable to quell the hurt, anger, or fear that arises. We even believe that the other person controls our feelings. "She makes me angry, sad, happy, disappointed and horny!" Wait a minute — she can't make you feel a thing without some participation from you. Yes, each of us is influenced by others and sometimes even manipulated, but the more consciousness we have, and the more we practice emotional self-soothing and skill building, the more control we have over our behaviors and attitudes. Automatic reactions can usually be slowed down and transformed into conscious choices and responses.

So Where Do Feelings Really Come From? Let's Ask Ms. Science...

On the physical level, feelings are a series of chemical and brain wave activities that sometimes have physiological outcomes such as tears or raised blood pressure. On the psychological level, feelings come from our own split-second interpretations of an experience. Sometimes we attribute responsibility of our feelings to someone else, as in "You made me angry." Even if we may have reactions (emotional or physiological) that are out of our conscious control, no one can "make us" behave a certain way. There are some circumstances such as physical coercion, battering, emotional abuse, brainwashing or torture which will erode our self-will and create a situation where control is extremely limited. Such circumstances create incentive or serious consequences that are impossible to avoid, and yet we always have some choice in our responses to a situation. Sometimes this choice may simply be to cultivate a different attitude toward a situation that seems unchangeable. When the situation is not safe or healthy we can cultivate an attitude that will help us get out.

What about our automatic reactions? During a conflict we often feel the need to explain and defend, or leave (emotionally or physically). These reactions have to do with our "fight, flight or freeze" responses to a perceived or actual threat (we may perceive situations as dangerous to us or to the stability of our relationship when they aren't). Our perceptions of what is happening in a conflict are learned from both early childhood experiences, and subsequent adult experiences. It has been shown that when a perceived or real threat exists we have a physiological response in which pulse rate increases and other physiological changes take place. At a 10% increase in pulse rate, we no longer have access to fully rational thinking (John M. Gottman, PhD). We react instead of respond. Slowing down the interaction, or taking a complete break is necessary to calm down our physiological arousal and allow access to rational thought.

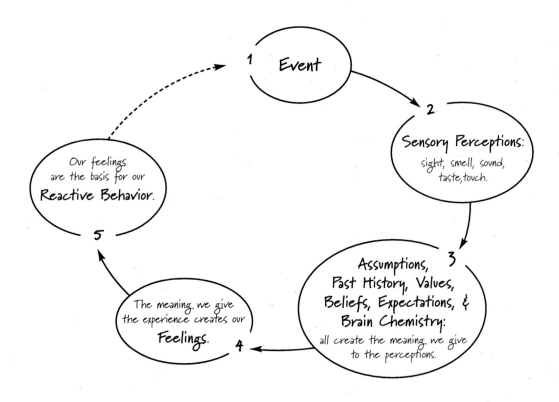

How Are Feelings & Reactions Created?

1. Event: You and your partner are talking and have different opinions about the subject. She scowls.

2. Perception: You see the muscles in her face shift into a recognizable pattern.

3. Assumptions/History: In a nano-second and underneath your conscious awareness your emotional mind "remembers" that whenever your father/mother/teacher was angry s/he scowled at you. This was usually followed by something unpleasant (e.g. disapproval, punishment).

4. Feelings: You feel threatened and scared, then angry.

5. Reactions: You react defensively, either leaving the scene, attacking verbally or justifying your position further.

Later you may find out that her scowl meant she was confused about something you said, or frustrated, or perhaps she had an itch on her forehead. A mistaken unconscious assumption or belief can skew an entire interaction.

Remember Dinah and Melody and their coming out compromises in Chapter 6? Melody felt more comfortable being out to people right away and Dinah wanted more contact before coming out. That wasn't their only difference. Melody was convinced that Dinah made her feel like an intellectual washout. Dinah loves to read and enjoys discussing ideas. She can find something of interest in any topic and she's well-read. This was very attractive to Mel when they first met, but after a year of being together Melody felt dull and tongue-tied in comparison. Being gregarious by nature, this was difficult for her. Melody had rarely found herself at a loss for words before. She first secretly resented Dinah as a show-off, and then openly blamed her bright beloved for making her feel stupid in front of others.

At this, Dinah got defensive. But later she was able to take a deep breath and listen to Melody's feelings. She asked Melody to explain why she thought she looked stupid when they were with others. Mel admitted she wasn't sure that others thought she looked stupid but that she herself thought she looked stupid.

They continued to talk and Mel bravely identified a few other assumptions that were in operation. She assumed that if she wasn't talking and interacting with people they would think she was dull, boring and stupid; that if people didn't say she was bright and witty that they thought she was dull, boring and stupid; that if they thought that, then it meant she was dull, boring and stupid; that if she knew eight things about kangaroos and someone else — especially Dinah — knew nine things about kangaroos, that meant that Mel was stupid and Dinah was smart. There were others, but it became evident that Dinah was not the culprit making Melody feel stupid. There were many assumptions and beliefs in operation that had nothing to do with Dinah. Realizing this gave Melody the opportunity to change them. As difficult as that was, it was a heck of a lot easier and more effective to change her beliefs and assumptions than to try and change Dinah! Once it became clear what the thoughts and assumptions were, Mel realized she didn't agree with them.

In order to change automatic reactions you must pay close attention to what goes on internally and slow down the response process. Only then can you apply your intellect (rational thought). You can do this by taking some deep breaths and waiting to speak. Ask yourself key questions: What am I feeling now? What story am I telling myself about this situation? What assumptions am I making? Check out those assumptions with your partner. Be curious about her answers. Doing this will begin to help you get clear, stay present and have many more choices about the outcome of the interaction.

Exercise 37 — Beliefs and Assumptions = Feelings   ♀

1. Identify a regular activity. Examples might include: going to the movies, washing the dishes, using your major mode of transportation, working, reading a newspaper, seeing people you know well on the street — got the idea?

2. Identify specific feelings you have about that situation or activity. List them all regardless of intensity, whether they are mutually exclusive and whether you like them or not. Examples might include excitement, dread, curiosity, resignation, concern, fear, happiness, guilt, depression, sadness, frustration, relief, pride, anger, shame, embarrassment, delight.

3. Identify your beliefs, thoughts and assumptions about this activity. For example, going to the movies is...fun and entertaining, a waste of time and money, not worth it unless it's really good film, is a risk of disappointment because of the roles women are usually given, a great escape, a good opportunity to consume expensive junk food and treats. Include as many thoughts and assumptions as you can identify, whether you believe they are rational or not.

Pause & Reflect

4. Which thoughts or assumptions result in which feelings? Match them up.

5. Experiment with changing one of your thoughts or assumptions even if you have to pretend to believe something different. Example: Change "Going to the movies is a waste of time" to "Going to the movies helps me relax."

6. Notice what happens to your feelings as you change your thought or assumption. Identify the new feelings.

Ineffective Models From the Past

We all grew up learning rules about communication. Many of these rules were unspoken, but, being clever children, we picked them up by observation. What we learn in childhood doesn't necessarily work in adulthood. Some family rules about communication prove to be blocks to healthy relating in our later years. These rules (like "crying is a weakness," "it's not worth much if you have to ask for it" and "don't let anyone know how you really feel") become incorporated into our relating systems as beliefs. These rules may have been absolutely necessary to survive in your family system but they may sabotage more open and healthy relating in your life now. Besides these "rules," we've also absorbed ineffective ways of communication from friends, teachers, religious leaders, TV, movies, and on from there.

Here's an example of old beliefs influencing interactions.

Melody grew up with three active and competitive siblings who jostled, cajoled and scrapped to improve or protect their position in the family pecking order. Knowing things and proving oneself "right" was basis for being top dog — just as not knowing and being proven "wrong" was basis for lowliness and being judged as stupid. Given the highly competitive atmosphere, there was little appreciation and few compliments. Respect and admiration were shown by agreeing with someone. Questioning someone or presenting another opinion was a way to bump someone out of their "position." As an adult, Mel's attitudes about her friends were much more generous and gracious, yet these old beliefs were just under the surface. They showed up most when she was dealing with Dinah, causing her to compete for being right when there was a difference of opinion or need. In order to end this particular form of conflict that arose Mel consciously checked out her assumptions and reminded herself that she didn't really value this kind of arguing anymore. This thinking began to lessen the strong influence those old beliefs had on her. Changes did not happen overnight. She gradually decided that her worth as a person was not based on how much she knew or on being right all of the time — a big relief to all involved (particularly Dinah!)

EXERCISE 38 — Blasts from the Past

---

1. What are the ineffective models of communication demonstrated by important people in your past?

   Some common examples: leaving the scene, being easily distracted, angry outbursts, glaring looks, blaming, withdrawing into silence, watching TV, overdrinking, overeating, abusing prescription or non-prescription drugs, overworking, changing the subject, placating (being falsely agreeable), throwing things, using threats, hitting/shoving, name calling, or using sarcasm.

2. Are you copying any of these today? Circle those.

Pause & Reflect

Exercise 39 — Problematic Thinking ♀

Here is a list of common false beliefs that wreak havoc with clear communication:

If you have to ask for it, it's not worth much.
If you ask for it, you're selfish or greedy.
Crying is a weakness.
Crying is a manipulation.
Don't let anyone know how you really feel.
If someone really loves you they will know what you want or need.
I know how she feels whether she says so or not.
I know her better than she knows herself.
I know what's best for her.
Saying you're sorry means you've lost.
Forgiving someone means you condone what they did.
If it's said as a joke you shouldn't get hurt or angry.
Being vulnerable is dangerous, it will be used against you.
You should always be in control of your feelings.
You can get someone to do what you want if you ask for it the right way.

1. Check off the ones that apply to you.

2. Add any of yours that are not listed.

3. Pick one of your beliefs and write about it, answering these questions:
    a. How did you learn this belief?

    b. What are the positive and negative results of using this belief?

    c. How can you change this belief to help your relationship?

Cultural, Regional and Generational Differences

Some communication styles are unique to our particular cultural or regional roots, our class background, or to our generation. The more extreme these differences are between partners, the broader the potential communication gap.

Here is an example of two different family styles influenced by both educational experience and culture.

Dinah's family read and discussed many topics. Offering different ideas, being persuasive and using supporting information were considered desirable skills. Engaging in serious or humorous conversation signified respect and regard. Quiet contemplation was considered an honorable activity as well. Education was highly valued. Emphasis was placed on decorum and being "appropriate." Anything louder than an excited conversational tone was considered offensive.

As you can guess, Dinah's rules for effective and acceptable communication were quite different from Mel's. In Mel's family, volume was considered an important communication tool — generally the more it was used the more assured the speaker was of being heard. There were exceptions, but this was standard operating procedure. These exchanges could be humorous, affectionate, playful, angry, frustrated, joyful, or any combination. They were guaranteed to be lively. Being quiet for any length of time indicated that someone didn't feel well, was a little slow or wasn't to be trusted. Emotional expression and engaging performance were valued over intellect or logic.

Exercise 40 — Cultural Influences ♀

1. What are your ways of communicating that are influenced by your cultural or regional roots, your class/educational background, or generation?

2. How do you think your partner's communication is affected by her cultural or regional roots, class/educational background, or generation?

3. List the differences and commonalities you have with your partner regarding cultural or regional roots, class/educational background, or generation.

Defensive Patterns

Fight or flight responses are instinctive to our species. They are a reaction to perceived or actual danger and serve to increase our chances of staying alive. Defensive responses such as fight or flight behaviors do communicate but don't effectively promote understanding or mutual resolution, so they are not very functional to protecting the relationship. Our fear emotions (abandonment, loss, shame and overwhelm) don't know the difference between this immediate distress and truly life-threatening circumstances. Most interactions with our partners are not issues of physical survival, however since primary interdependent partnerships enhance our survival chances, when a primary bond feels threatened a "hard wired" emotional alarm sounds. This emotional alarm sends us into immediate defensive reaction.

Modern fighting and fleeing take many forms including: emotional and/or physical explosions, throwing things, name calling, running away, emotional shutdown, the silent treatment, changing the subject. Passive-aggressive behaviors are a combination of both fight and flight. Someone who employs this defensive pattern appears to be innocent while really being hostile. These behaviors include being sarcastic, patronizing, using disguised jabs and put-downs, conspicuous incompetence and passive resistance.

EXERCISE 41 — I Will Defend to the Death!

Think back to your childhood. What were the defensive patterns used in your family in times of conflict?

1. Which patterns did the adults in your household have?

2. Siblings?

Pause & Reflect

3. What were your usual defensive/protective patterns as a child?

4. How about now, as an adult?

Addictions and Substance Abuse

Another flight response can be the use and/or abuse of substances such as alcohol, drugs, or food, or compulsive activities such as workaholism, gambling, or sex. Any or all of these can be used to avoid uncomfortable or overwhelming feelings. Much has been written about the effects of addictions on both individuals and couples. Very simply, any interference in a person's ability to be conscious of her feelings and rational in her thought processes means that communication is at best erratic and reactive. If addiction is a factor in your relationship, it must be addressed. It is difficult to successfully communicate with anyone who is actively under the influence of an addictive substance or engaged in a compulsive activity. When this situation arises, it is best to postpone the discussion until both parties have returned to sobriety and/or emotional equilibrium.

EXERCISE 42 — Under the Influence ♀

1. Identify ways that alcohol/substance abuse or compulsive activities affect your communication with your partner.

Resolving Communication Blocks

Now that we've focused on problems in communication, we turn to solutions. What follows are several tools, methods and perspectives that facilitate good communication and prosperous relating.

Active Listening

The following communication process is one that promotes and develops compassion and empathy, self-control and containment, honesty and self-revealing. It is an ongoing practice, and when used will encourage deep understanding and foster emotionals bonds.

This is a developed version of "Active Listening" that asks you to go beyond routine repetition, fault finding or justification, and help each other discover the feelings and beliefs beneath the defenses.

Active listening is a seemingly simple process, but a difficult one to master. (A better name perhaps would be "Focused Listening and Insightful Speaking.") By using it you can actually avoid years — yes, years — of suffering between two people. With regular use, your relationship will be more satisfying than you ever imagined. A hard sell? Perhaps, yet personal and professional experience demonstrates that these are not empty promises.

Abby and Paula Demonstrate Their Skill at Active Listening

Abby brings up an issue she's having with Paula. Since it's her issue she is the Speaker first and Paula is the Listener.

> Abby: "I felt hurt and rejected when I found out there was a big event at your job and you didn't tell me. I'd really like you to feel comfortable, and want to share that information with me."

> Paula: "You felt hurt and left out when I didn't tell you about the event at work and you want me to tell you about everything that happens there."

> Abby: "Not quite. I don't mean that you should tell me everything that happens at work. I wish you would want to tell me about events that I might be included in."

> Paula: "Okay, you wish I really wanted to talk with you about work events, not to feel like I have to."

> Abby: "Yes."

> Paula: "If I wanted to share this information with you what would that mean to you?"

> Abby: "It would mean to me that you really trusted me, that you cared enough about me to include me in your decision making."

> Paula: "So you would feel trusted and cared about if I included you in work events?"

> Abby: "Well yes, that would be true, but it's not what I meant. I would feel trusted and cared about if you shared your process about whether we should go or not."

> Paula: "So what's really important to you is that I tell you more about what I'm thinking?"

> Abby: "Yes."

Paula: "And when you found out about the work event, and I hadn't mentioned it to you, your feelings got hurt…(contemplating). I can really see how that might have been painful for you."

Abby: (Sigh of relief.) "Yes."

Now Paula Asks For a Turn as Speaker

Paula: "I feel real uncomfortable with the idea of our going to events at my job. I was afraid that you'd be upset if we didn't go, so I didn't mention it. I'd like to be able to talk about those events without any pressure to do anything."

Abby: "You felt afraid I'd be upset if you didn't want to go to work events with me. You feel uncomfortable about us going to them and want to be able to talk about them without any pressure from me to do something."

Paula: "Yes."

Abby: "Do you experience me pressuring you to make decisions before you're ready?"

Paula: "Sometimes, but mostly I'm unhappy with myself for worrying about what my co-workers think."

And the talk continues. As each woman feels understood and not judged, her willingness to take a deeper look at what she's experiencing and take responsibility for it increases. This decreased defensiveness allows for acceptance which in turn helps each woman feel safer and more connected to the other.

Looks like it might be easy, perhaps even boring or contrived? But it's harder than you think to stay in a non-defensive, exploratory mode. Take your time reading the instructions below, have them in front of you to refer to the first few tries.

To Begin:

  ▼ make an agreement with your partner to spend a half hour practicing this form of communication

  ▼ chose a time and place when you won't be interrupted and are reasonably rested and fed

  ▼ alternate between listener and speaker

  ▼ set a time limit for each person's turn

Listener's Objective

Your primary objective is to understand and empathize with what your partner has to say. Not just the words but the feelings that go with them and the perceptions that created those feelings.

In order to do this you must set your intention towards this goal and keep reminding yourself that this is what you want and intend to do.

Pause & Reflect

How Do You Achieve This Objective?

▼ Turn your attention to your partner. Hold your judgments, reactions and brilliant problem-solving abilities in a temporary resting state for safekeeping.

▼ As she talks, listen — really focus on what she is saying. If your mind wanders or starts to make up a reply bring your attention back to her.

▼ At this time do not give her feedback on what she says.

▼ An occasional, "uh huh," or otherwise encouraging gesture such as a head nod is useful to let her know you're on task and she's coming through clearly. Ask for clarification if need be.

▼ You do not need to get upset. It's up to you to calm any reactivity that arises on your part.

▼ You do not need to agree with what she is saying. This in not about finding an "objective truth."

▼ Attempt to hear the feelings behind the statements.

▼ Suspend judgment and problem-solving — don't defend yourself, argue or cross complain.

▼ Every few paragraphs repeat back what you've heard her say to show understanding.

▼ Use your own words or her words but say them with comprehension — you are not a robot.

▼ Your partner then amends and corrects any misinformation. Accept amendments and corrections at face value.

▼ You repeat the correction. Your intention is to imagine what it is like to be her, having her particular experience, not what *you* would do/feel in her place.

- ▼ Remember that what she says is information about her, not you, try not to take it personally.

- ▼ Don't look for solutions until later, and then only if she wants solutions.

- ▼ Do this until she's finished or your agreed-upon time limit has been met.

Ask Questions

Develop an interested and curious state of mind. (Sometimes pretending to be an investigative reporter helps.) Ask questions when something isn't quite clear or when you can get her to talk more fully about the topic. The questions you ask need to be designed to understand your partner's experience, not challenge it or lead her in a certain direction. Can you come up with any examples of your own that will let your partner know you really understand?

> *Reminder to Self —*
> *Am I in a place to listen with openness? I do not own this problem. I do not need*
> *to get upset. It's up to me to manage my reactions.*

Empathize

Do your best to put yourself in your partner's shoes. Respond with empathy or compassion. Keep making empathic statements until a soothing moment occurs. You don't have to agree with her perspective to have empathy for her experience. You can hold onto yourself and still be able to imagine what it's like for the other person.

> *Reminder to Self —*
> *My partner is a separate person with her own feelings, thoughts, personality and family history. I only need to listen, not to look for solutions.*

Speaker's Objective

> *Your primary objective is to look deeply within yourself to explore*
> *and reveal your feelings, thoughts and your perspective to your*
> *partner without blame.*

> *In order to do this you must set your intention towards this goal*
> *and keep reminding yourself that this is what you want and*
> *intend to do.*

Pause & Reflect

How Do You Achieve This Objective?

- First get clear on your main concern.

- Check your partner's availability (emotionally, physically). Is she ready to hear you?

- Focus on one topic/issue at a time. Stay on track.

- Keep your statements clear, simple and direct.

- Communicate and own how you feel about a particular situation and what you'd like or want. Express contradictory or mixed feelings if there are any.

- Explore the layers of feelings beneath the surface. Allow yourself to experience your vulnerability.

- Use "I" statements. (See below for examples of "I" statements.)

- Avoid blaming, accusing, name calling or lecturing.

- Make sure you stop often (for some it's OK to stop every few paragraphs, others may need you to stop every few sentences) and give her time to tell you what she understands you to be saying.

- Listen to what your partner heard.

- Provide any corrections or amendments.

Revealing One's Self

Feelings are often complex and can even be contradictory. Go beyond simply expressing one feeling. Look for the vulnerability that may be underneath your initial feeling ... e.g. sadness, fear, jealousy, hurt, guilt, etc.

> *Reminder to Self —*
> *This is my problem. It's an expression of who I am. It's about me revealing myself and being willing to express my own thoughts and feelings.*

Be Open to Self-discovery

Explore your personal, inner experience. Keep going deeper into how you feel and why those feelings developed. What does this tell you about yourself, how you respond, how you think and the beliefs and assumptions you have made?

> *Reminder to Self —*
> *This process is about my willingness to take a risk to speak or discover my truth, and about increasing my ability to tolerate the expression of our differences.*

Using "I Statements"

"I statements" are a form of sentence that communicates your experience without blame, radically reducing the likelihood that you will get a defensive response. Use I statements liberally in your daily life and they will come easily when practicing active listening.

Examples of What They Are:

"I feel (sad, excited, confused, happy, etc.) about _____."

"When you do/say _____ I tell myself that you mean _____ and I feel _____."

"I'm struggling with something that happened the other day. I'm feeling pissed about _____ and I want to lash out. I'm really hurt by what I perceive as your attitude. I find myself blaming you. I'd like to feel better but I can't get there yet."

Examples of What They Are Not:

"I feel hurt when you are mean and judgmental." (This is blaming and it pronounces how the other person is behaving rather than revealing what their behavior meant to you.)

"I think you're a fool for being her friend." (This is a blatant criticism without taking responsibility for the judgement.)

"I feel you are stupid for turning down that job." (This is a put down in the disguise of a "feeling.")

"I feel you're wrong." (This is a thought, not a feeling. Thoughts can be backed up by logic and in the case of an outright disagreement will need to be explained. Feelings don't necessarily have logical explanations and are important in understanding a persons perspective. They are usually only one word.)

OK, now it's your turn. Try it — just try it. There is nothing quite like the deep joy of really feeling known by the person you care about and who you hope cares about you. Once this tool becomes readily accessible through practice, it's use can flow more naturally. You will receive lifelong benefits from your efforts.

EXERCISE 43 — Focused Listening & Insightful Speaking*

* aka "Active Listening"

1. Select a neutral topic and exchange messages using active listening and "I" messages.

2. If you're ready to take on more of a challenge, have another go using a more charged topic where there are differences of perspective.

NOTE: If it is impossible to resist giving judgments or opinions, or if one of you feels blamed or judged in spite of wonderful "I" statements, leave it for now and try it again later with a less charged topic. As you become more advanced in using this tool you may be capable of self identifying your own slips (blaming, judging, giving advice.) You can save a conversation and avoid a fight. If you feel blamed or judged you may be capable of using an "I" statement to say so in a non-accusatory way. If these all escape you — take a break. When you're both ready, try again.

Compromise and Collaboration

Compromise and collaboration make differences in style, needs, wants and even temperament more tolerable. Compromise means getting some of what we want enough of the time to be livable. It requires clearly knowing and expressing what we need and want, and negotiating with our partners about those needs and desires. Compromise enables us to find release from immediate power struggles. Even more important, it enables us to build and maintain trust and good will in our relationships. When we take risks and learn the value of compromising, it is easier to tolerate the disappointment of not getting everything we want all of the time.

121

Mel and Di first had to listen to one another to reach a workable solution to their different needs regarding being out in Chapter 6. They came to respect their contrasting perspectives, feelings and needs. They also had to truly desire a compromise that could bridge those differences before being able to develop an acceptable option. After a few successful outcomes they started feeling good about their ability to compromise and used those abilities more. Dinah found that accommodating her partner's desire to be more "out" in the world didn't mean that she would always feel exposed and vulnerable. She could set the limits she really needed even if they weren't always ideal. Melody realized that she had a greater degree of freedom than she had assumed and came to value the use of discrimination. She realized she still had choices.

Exercise 44 — At the Bargaining Table (or Negotiation 101)

(This is an involved exercise, but it can be very fruitful. If it sounds overwhelming and too business-like, take a big breath and start with one step at a time. You, too/two can negotiate your way to satisfaction. If you get stuck, find yourself swamped with emotional responses, or can't find anything to negotiate or agree about, take a break. When you've both had time to reflect, or when emotions have been sorted try it again. Take breathers whenever you need them. Remember, relating is a process — doing it well is just as valuable as the end results.)

1. Identify an area where you and your lover have different needs and/or styles. (For instance, how much time you spend with friends, use of the shared car, parenting, housework).

2. Select a situation where your preferences are mutually exclusive, i.e., if you get your way she doesn't get hers, or vice versa.

3. Describe how you feel about the current situation while the other person actively listens. Then reverse roles.

4. Describe how you would like the situation to be different, or remain the same, while the other actively listens. Then reverse roles.

5. Write the four lists below and take turns sharing them with each other:

   No-Problem Items: These are the ways you are willing and able to comply with your partner's preferences right now — in fact, you may think they are good ideas that you were about to suggest.

   Trade Items: These are the ways you are willing to adapt if your partner can meet some of your preferences. List what you are willing to do and what you'd like in trade.

   Future Options: These are her preferences that you are willing to consider meeting in the future, if particular factors change. Describe the factors you need to be different, if you know them.

   Bottom-Line Items: These are non-negotiable requirements that you can't imagine living without (or with).

6. Review your lists and proceed with the following:

   a. Select and mark "no-problem" items you agree on.

   b. Identify and mark trade items and negotiate until the trade is acceptable enough that both of you are willing to try it.

   c. Determine the beginning and ending dates of a trial period.

   d. Write the negotiated compromise below.

7. Review your "future options" and "bottom-line" items. As best as you can, honestly assess whether your "bottom-lines" are tolerable today. If they are not, review again to see if any "bottom line" can be moved to possible "future options."

Tolerance

We are all unique, as people and as lesbians. Differences don't mean that two people can't be quite happy together. Differences are always part of our attraction to others. They are a source of richness in our relationships. Differences in lesbian relationships can sometimes be perceived as quite threatening to the "us against the world" stand that homophobia can evoke. Most differences between partners are more easily tolerated if they are not perceived as threats to the relationship or to the individuals.

Tolerance means allowing (putting up with) or respecting another's beliefs and/or practices without sharing them. Tolerance allows flexibility and space for differences, without threatening the fundamental connection in the relationship.

EXERCISE 45 — Practicing Tolerance   ♀/♀♀

1. Choose one of your partner's behaviors or characteristics that you don't care for and which is not likely to change.

2. Make a commitment to tolerate it for a week.

3. Notice the effects of your tolerating this behavior (not commenting or expressing distress in any way, self-soothing your negative feelings). Ask yourself if you could begin to accept it.

Pause & Reflect

4. If the behavior remains unacceptable, use active listening to describe the effects of the behavior on you, then try negotiation to see if an acceptable change can be made. Remember that characteristics and many behaviors are not easy for an individual to change, even when she wants to. By simply appreciating and praising the behaviors you like and ignoring the ones you don't you begin to set up a change. Nagging **never** works.

Autonomy

Autonomy is the ability to stand on your own, have your own opinions and abilities and to be self-governing. While cooperation and connectedness are essential in relationship, autonomy gives relationship its maturity and depth. There are many positive aspects to being different from our partner. These differences make our lives challenging but also interesting. Many of the challenging characteristics our partner exhibits are actually aspects of ourselves that we have ignored or that need cultivating. Differences remind us that we are separate people even in a close relationship. Being reminded of our separateness can be comforting, appealing, freeing, frightening, or even depressing, depending on the meaning we give it. Personal boundaries and a sense of self are blurred when we confuse what others think and feel with what is true for us. It is important to remember that other people's perspectives, opinions and even judgments are primarily information about them *even if we are the topic.* It is only when we can see the other person as separate from us that we can be objective about the messages they give us and it is only then that we can really experience who the other person is and who we are.

Healthy autonomy enhances a relationship as each person brings outside interests and values to the table. Without autonomy we lose perspective of the bigger picture of our lives and depend too much on our partner for a sense of self. Ironically, an authentic self can only truly be expressed when both women feel secure and loved.

Exercise 46 — I've Got to Be Me!   ♀

1. List several ways in which you feel autonomous from your partner.

2. Do these feel like positive choices? If not, invent some ways that you can be autonomous which are positive choices.

3. List several things you do independent of your partner that make you feel good about yourself.

4. Describe an interest you have separate from your partner that you could cultivate more fully.

Taking It Personally

How many times have you heard someone say, "Don't take it so personally"? Unfortunately, this is often said as a defensive statement after some mean-spirited remark or deed. Setting that aside for the moment what does "Don't take it so personally" really mean and why can that be a key to successful relating? It means that much of what someone says is really a comment on them, it may sound like a statement about you, it may even be intended as statement about you, but in fact it reflects much about the speaker; their mood, their beliefs and world view, their needs and expectation, and their past relationship experience. If, when confronted with a remark that bothers us, we could step back a bit and remember this, then we would be less upset and able to hear and respond more clearly. We would have less need to defend ourselves, try to change the other person's mind or control their behavior, because we would not be as affected. Then we could actually take care of ourselves better. This does not absolve us (the listener), however, from taking into consideration what is being said and taking responsibility for our part in whatever issue is discussed.

"Not taking it personally" is a skill-set that is ever evolving. Another word for "Not taking things personally" is "detaching." In order to get a more complete idea of this concept read on.

Loving Detachment

Detachment is a perspective that allows us to be responsible for our own experience and welfare. It enables us to make decisions without the ulterior motive of manipulating others or fearing their reaction. Using detachment we can allow the other person to have her own experience separate and different from ours, even when it is difficult for us to do.

Suzanne and Karen

Suzanne is in the fashion industry. Karen is a co-owner of a computer store. They've been a couple for five years. Karen has a business partner, Phyllis, and they have enjoyed vigorous success in their business venture from its inception seven years ago. However, in the past three years their different styles and visions of where to go with the business have resulted in deeper and deeper conflicts. What was once a congenial, exciting and satisfying work relationship has become a source of anxiety and frustration for Karen.

Karen's usually easygoing demeanor has become interspersed with long periods of silent withdrawal and emotional unavailability at home — much to Suzanne's distress. Suzanne actually prefers the occasional episodes when Karen is unable to contain her anger and frustration and rants and raves about how upset she is with Phyllis. It is at those times that Suzanne is more successful in maintaining her objectivity, practicing active listening and providing emotional support. Both women seem to experience more closeness and engagement as a result of these conversations.

During these conversations about Karen's business Suzanne struggles not to give detailed directives or advice about the business. Sometimes she can't resist. Sure enough, Karen is defensive of her partnership with Phyllis, reminding Suzanne of how long and hard she and Phyllis have worked together, reminding Suzanne of her limited perspective. ("No one who hasn't had their own business can really understand.")

Suzanne knows that an ability to remain detached is more productive. When her unhappiness with Karen's withdrawal escalates to resentment and anger, her ability to detach fades accordingly. At these times, blame, hurt and anger are intermingled with her brilliant common-sense solutions.

As for Karen, her opportunities to practice detachment come both at work and at home. When Karen listens to Suzanne's feelings about the business, it is a challenge for her to hear them as Suzanne's experience and not as criticism and blame. When she is detached she can hear and consider Suzanne's insights and judge for herself which ones have merit and which ones don't fit for her circumstances. She can see the business situation as just that, a situation, rather than as an obvious sign that she is a failure.

LOVING DETACHMENT IS:	IS NOT:
allowing her to have her own feelings and opinions	acting judgmental or superior
taking care of yourself	acting without regard for the other
recognizing you're not responsible for everything	becoming blaming or dismissive
letting go of obsessing	shutting down of all feelings
staying present and witnessing her feelings and perspectives, not interjecting yours	becoming emotionally withdrawn or aloof
remembering her behavior is not a reflection on you	denying your own part in the issue being raised
offering one's skills and support without attachment to outcome	trying to "fix it" and getting mad if they don't use your advice or help
making peace with what's out of your control	being uncaring

EXERCISE 47 — Detach with Love ♀

1. Describe a situation in which your partner or friend is involved that is worrisome to you.

2. List your concerns.

3. Write about how the various outcomes and/or problems would or do affect you.

4. For those aspects of the situation that do not significantly affect you, it is time to employ detachment. Use some "self talk" (thoughts to repeat to yourself) to help stay detached, such as: "This is her issue, not mine"; "It's OK to let her work this out herself"; "I can listen without getting involved"; "Don't give advice"; "I don't need to fix it"; "What she does is not a reflection on me"; or any other helpful phrases that keep you from getting pulled into the fray.

5. It is valuable for you to discuss with your partner or friend the parts that significantly affect you, letting her know about the aspects that relate only to you. This is a time for employing active listening and, possibly, negotiation.

Assertiveness

Assertive and clear communication allows individuals to know and seek their needs in ways that are in accord with the health of the relationship. Assertiveness is responsible self-expression. It can include limit-setting, saying no and expressions of anger. It can mean reaching out, being affectionate and sharing positive feelings. It can mean taking the lead in an endeavor, asking for something you want or need and holding up your part in a negotiation. Being assertive expresses an attitude of self-respect, as well as respect for others and the relationship. It is genuine and responsible self-expression. It is a demonstration of belief that others can take care of themselves if you are forthright and genuine. As stated previously, all communication involves more than just the words. Communicating assertively relays self confidence by the way you hold your body, your gestures, facial expressions, voice tone, and timing.

Many people confuse assertiveness with aggression. Assertiveness is not bullying or insisting, it is not being self-righteous or acting superior. The chart that follows outlines the differences between passive, assertive and aggressive behavior.

PASSIVE BEHAVIOR	ASSERTIVE BEHAVIOR	AGGRESSIVE BEHAVIOR
keeps thoughts & feelings inside	expresses thoughts & feelings constructively	expresses thoughts & feelings destructively
allows others to choose for you	chooses for self	chooses for others
does not get what she wants except by accident or manipulation	a better chance that she will get what she wants	may get what she wants by hurting or threatening others
feels hurt, anxious & powerless	feels good about self	feels (either or all) victimized, powerful, remorseful

Patsy, Ardith and Annie

Three friends want to go on a canoe trip together. They each have the task of discussing it with their respective partners. Their styles are very different.

Patsy Passive waits until her lover is in a great mood (this doesn't happen until two days before the trip). She says: "Honey? Do we still have those waterproof stuff bags from our rafting trip three years ago? You know I really miss those outdoor trips. Didn't you go canoeing in Boundary Waters just last year? You know Annie and Ardith are going canoeing this weekend. Just a quick trip, only four days. You were gone three weeks weren't you? Oh no, I guess it was just two. It's been so long since I've been away on a fun trip. We did go see your family last winter, but that was when your grandmother died. In fact, things have been so hard for you lately, wouldn't you like to have a break? If I got out of your way this weekend you could have the whole house to yourself. I know you've been wanting to turn your new stereo up all the way and really rock out. What do you think? Wouldn't you like that?"

Ardith Aggressive comes home after talking with Patsy and Annie, walks in the house and says: "I'm going on a canoe trip in two weeks. I know I said I'd go to that damn communications class with you, but I never really wanted to do that. Besides, I know how to communicate just fine. Don't get bent out of shape about this, I know how emotional you are. You do the things that really matter to you. Now it's my turn. So where's my new paddle?"

Annie Assertive comes home and asks her partner if she has some time to talk. Her partner is busy right then and they agree to talk when she's finished. Annie says: "I just saw Ardith and Patsy. We thought it would be great fun to do a canoe trip in two weeks. The idea appeals to me and I'd really like to go. I don't think we had any plans that weekend. What are your thoughts and feelings about this? Oh, you're right, we did say we'd clean out the garage together. Could we do that the weekend before or after the trip? How about that?"

131

EXERCISE 48 — Stating Your Case ♀

1. Pick a request or need you'd like to communicate to your partner (or make one up).

2. Write the three different approaches you could take to your situation.

    Passive

    Aggressive

    Assertive

Pause & Reflect

Exercise 49 — Acting It Out: On Stage At Home   ♀/♀♀

1. With your partner, act out fictional requests or proposals using passive, assertive and aggressive methods of communication.

2. Choose one of you to be the speaker/performer first, the other is the listener/audience. After you do a round, trade off roles.

3. As the speaker/performer, stay as faithful to each character as you can.

4. As the listener/audience, note to yourself how you feel in response to your partner's approach and imagine your likely verbal and/or behavioral responses. Describe your responses to your partner when she's finished with each of her performances. Be as specific as you can about your feelings and thoughts.

5. After you've done the "practice/acting" each identify a genuine request or proposal you've made or want to make with your partner. Each of you should have a different request or proposal.

6. Now present your genuine request/proposal to one another using an assertive approach.

7. Discuss how you feel about the proposals and proceed to negotiation or agreement.

Giving Good Feedback

There are times when each of us feels critical of our partners and friends. There are times when we think if only they'd listen to reason, all would be well. Or if only they'd do it "this" way things would turn out right. No relationship (that I know of) is entirely free of critical thought. Some of these thoughts are best kept to yourself (perhaps most of them), but when there is a persistent problem that affects you adversely it is best to speak up about it. If you want a good result then skill is necessary. Feedback about a problem area can backfire into a full blown fight, be silently ignored or deeply hurtful. Or it can become an informative discussion, an intimate confession or a cooperative negotiation. It depends a lot on whether it is "good feedback."

What is good feedback? A pie in the face is certainly effective feedback — it has a definite effect. But does it have the effect you want? If you want to elicit shock, hurt, anger, fear or retaliation and defensiveness, then you've succeeded. If not, then a pie in the face is not the kind of feedback you want to use. (Projectile pies aren't considered sweet feedback by most recipients.) Feedback can range from criticism or the silent treatment to praise, prizes and adulation. In order for your gems of wisdom to be effective they must be useful to the recipient. That can't happen if you've alienated her.

If you want cooperation and respect, and want to provide information, to initiate lasting changes, to support self-esteem, and to build trust, you need to use the kind of feedback that will bring these results. It's good to use judgment, but not to be judgmental. Similarly, critical faculties are needed to make important choices, but it is rarely helpful to criticize.

Useful Feedback Is:

▾ Descriptive rather than evaluative or judgmental. By describing one's own reaction, the recipient is free to use it or not as she sees fit. Avoiding evaluative language reduces the need for the recipient to react defensively.

▾ Specific rather than general. To be told "you are dominating" will probably not be very useful (or well received). To be told "just now when we were deciding the issue I didn't think you listened to me and I felt forced to accept your argument or be attacked."

▾ Taking into account the needs of both the receiver and giver of feedback. Feedback can be destructive when it serves only one's own needs and fails to consider the needs of the recipient.

▾ Directed toward behavior which the receiver can do something about. Frustration is increased when a person is reminded of some short-coming without any idea as to how to go about about changing it.

- Most useful when it is solicited, when the receiver is open to it and sees it as well-intended. Unsolicited feedback, however, is sometimes necessary to communication as well.

- Well-timed. In general, feedback is most powerful at the earliest opportunity after the given occurrence (depending, of course, on the person's readiness to hear it, support available from others, etc.) Sometimes it is prudent or unavoidable to wait a time before giving feedback. This does not lessen it's usefulness.

- Appropriate to the situation. Feedback that is likely to be heard as negative is best given in private. Feedback that is likely to be heard as complimentary can usually be given either in public or private.

- Checked to ensure clear communication. One way of doing this is to have the receiver try to rephrase the feedback she has received to see if it corresponds to what the sender had in mind (active listening).

- Information about the speaker's direct experience with the recipient's behavior, not secondhand or hearsay.

If you've practiced all of the above and still find your communication breaking down into destructive tangles, consider some resources that might be of help. Individual and couples counseling can help sort out and resolve communication breakdowns that interfere with your relationship or your feeling overwhelmed. Read other books on communication to help you to get a broader perspective. Attend workshops and/or talks on communication and lesbian issues; these can help you improve your standards and skills. And talk to friends about their communication process. Share your experiences and offer each other feedback. Do this individually, and as a couple, if you can.

Conclusion: Raising the Bar

Speaking up — not simply blurting out your every thought or feeling — is a tall order. Each of us owes it to ourselves, our partners, friends and children to cultivate our inner awareness and an authentic voice of understanding, compassion and clarity. As women we are prone to mistaking more words for better communication, or expressing any feelings for true insight. This chapter can help you sort out what is authentic expression and what is reactive babel. If you set your own goals for communication (verbal and physical expressions) and return to them again and again, the quality of your relationship will increase. Do not wait for your partner, friend or parent to change. You change and the dynamic between you cannot remain stagnant. Delving deeply can be a risky business, but if deep connection with another is desired it is a risk worth taking.

Chapter 9

Fighting Fair

"It is not true that life is one damn thing after another...
it's one damn thing over and over."
EDNA SAINT VINCENT MILLAY

Is Conflict Normal?

Conflict between people exists when one or both feel threatened, or when their needs, wants or values are significantly different or mutually exclusive. Conflict is a natural part of being human. Conflict is often scary, but it is neither inherently good or bad. In fact, conflict can be useful. It is complex, depending on the circumstances and the people involved.

Resolving conflict is a constant process in our daily lives. It's as normal as breathing. However, when we think of conflict, we usually think of fighting. Fortunately, we resolve hundreds of conflicts a day without fighting, from deciding who gets the last piece of pie in the fridge to relocating for a job opportunity. Conflicts are sometimes resolved without fighting by ignoring a situation; consciously letting the situation pass; choosing to follow rules; making concessions and compromises; taking turns; taking "space"; tolerating; sharing; flipping a coin; finding outside help; letting other forces (such as fate) decide; postponing decisions; and seeing the humor of a situation. And, of course, we also have fights. Each type of resolution has its "side-effects". One difference between a constructive and a destructive resolution to conflict is whether the people involved end up feeling respected or demeaned.

Constructive Responses to Conflict

Constructive responses to conflict take into account each persons emotional history and coping behaviors. They involve regulating one's own emotions in order to retain some rationality. And they require the ability to differentiate between what's your issue and what's my issue.

To interact well during times of conflict it is important to broaden one's view and remember that there is much more to the relationship than this problem, that emotions running high color what is said and intensify the experience.

To illustrate a successfully resolved conflict we introduce Nancy and Yvonne. Their conflict is minor but it's good for demonstrating some different elements involved in skilled resolution. These elements can be applied to much more serious conflicts. The more emotionally charged the problem the more difficult they are to apply.

Nancy is doing chores she has put off for weeks. She is looking forward to rewarding herself with the last piece of a cherry pie. She finally finishes rinsing out the garbage can. Coming indoors with satisfaction, she pulls off her grungy sweatshirt, washes up, puts on the tea kettle and opens the refrigerator to get that long-awaited piece of pie. Is it there? NO! She looks everywhere, rummaging past the mayonnaise and pickle jars, moving things aside. She opens the fruit and vegetable bins. Closing the door, she notices the crumb-crusted plate on the counter. "Where's my piece of cherry pie?" she exclaims. She whirls and stomps into the living room to confront her wicked, pie-snatching partner, Yvonne.

The stage is set. Nancy thought that last piece of pie was hers. It was a clearly saved leftover from two nights ago. She feels a right of ownership. Yvonne assumed whatever is in the fridge for more than a day is a mutually held resource to be consumed on a first-come, first-served basis.

▼ Constructive responses to conflict include acknowledging and accepting the differences
you and your partner have in values and preferences.

Nancy reminded Yvonne that two nights earlier Yvonne had eaten her own piece of pie. Nancy declared she was saving hers for the next day. She'd wrapped it in plastic and stored it in the fridge in front of Yvonne. Yvonne protested that that was two days ago and that "tomorrow" was yesterday.

138

▼ Constructive responses to conflict allow assumptions and expectations to be brought out into the open and their connection to present circumstances evaluated.

Yvonne reluctantly acknowledged witnessing such actions and declarations. Nancy acknowledged that two days had passed while she still believed she had first dibs on the pie. She contended, however, that Yvonne should have asked her before consuming it.

▼ In constructive responses, disappointments and responsibility are acknowledged as illusions fade.

Yvonne's family members always marked their "saved serving" of favorite foods. How was she supposed to remember that piece of pie was Nancy's? She asked if Nancy would be willing to use one of the blue plates when she wants to stash something she considers hers alone. Nancy agreed to do so only if Yvonne would swear not to touch anything so marked. Yvonne agreed.

▼ Constructive responses to conflict enable you and your partner to integrate your respective family-of-origin patterns into your current relationship.

Yvonne thought the pie was available. She understood Nancy's point of view when she remembered her partner's declaration. Yvonne offered to make a conciliatory peach cobbler. Their trust in their abilities to reach constructive resolutions were affirmed as they felt understood and a new food saving agreement was crafted.

▼ Constructive responses to conflict establish workable rules and guidelines for building and maintaining trust. We must be able to trust that we can meet enough of our individual needs while respecting the health and well-being of the relationship and the other person.

It is often easier to relinquish the last piece of pie than it is to let go of the position of "being right." However, neither Yvonne nor Nancy claimed absolute decision-making power. Both value a balance of power and shared solutions over rightful claim to the last piece of pie — which is quite mature of them.

▼ Constructive responses to conflict establish a balance of power.

Yvonne and Nancy were involved in defining the boundaries of what is whose, what is shared and how that is decided. Something more important than a piece of pie would be more emotionally charged and involve higher stakes, but the same issues would exist. Nancy and Yvonne went about constructing boundaries in ways that were tolerable and livable for them. Your definition of tolerable may be differ-

ent from hers. *The important thing is that the arrangements work for those who live with them.*

▼ Constructive responses to conflict establish a balance of autonomy and togetherness and set up boundaries that are tolerable and livable for all involved.

> *When Nancy confronted Yvonne she remembered Yvonne's sensitivity to shouting. Between the kitchen and living room she took a quick breath and was able to be respectful of Yvonne's limits about expressing anger. Without shouting she asserted what she perceived as her right of pie ownership. Yvonne acknowledged her memory lapse and successfully proposed a solution to help prevent such lapses. Yvonne offered compensation and Nancy graciously accepted.*

▼ Constructive responses to conflict enable partners to use and further develop their abilities to assert themselves and effectively negotiate mutually acceptable outcomes.

> *Nancy and Yvonne can trust each other to effectively speak up for themselves, to persevere through the process of negotiation, and to genuinely try to find mutually workable solutions.*

▼ Constructive response to conflict recognizes and values interdependence. We gain more through shared resources and efforts than always choosing solitary ownership and endeavors.

> *Nancy and Yvonne share many resources that made their negotiation successful, i.e., the ability to stay aware of the other's emotional history and limits, the skill to express feelings without blame, the willingness to compromise. They demonstrated valuing their interdependence rather than the use of arbitrary power.*

▼ Constructive responses to conflict make the process of synthesis possible.

> *Prior to this culinary incident Nancy and Yvonne had separate points of view regarding ownership of cherished leftovers. Through this interaction they sorted through their individual perspectives and built new mutual guidelines. They increased their conflict resolution skills by practicing them.*

When we have repeated arguments that end in frustration, hurt and regret, it's a sure bet that we are participating in a pattern of reactive feelings and behaviors that replay over and over again, only with different triggers or words. We get stuck in a destructive conflict loop that can only change if we can identify the pattern of reactiveness and the deeper feelings behind them.

If Nancy and Yvonne had not employed some awareness or ability to listen and take responsibility, each of them may have gotten stuck in just such a destructive loop. If Nancy had generalized and said, "There you go again, ignoring what I said and doing whatever *you* want. You really don't care about me at all." And Yvonne had replied, "Oh yeah, you just lay in wait, setting me up to make some little mistake, and then you pounce. I'm never good enough for you."

This would be the same basic fight they had when Yvonne locked the keys in the car and again when Nancy got mad at Yvonne for letting the campfire run down and again when Yvonne got mad at Nancy for telling her how to load the dishwasher.

Without being able to explore their vulnerabilities and reactive patterns, this loop could continue and become more deeply entrenched and hurtful over time.

It's fitting that the conflict stage comes after falling in love — if we weren't attached and enamored we'd never tolerate it. Recognizing differences and negotiating conflicts is necessary before true acceptance and collaboration can be very successful. Couples that attempt to proceed past the conflict stage without having mastered basic functional responses to conflict are asking too much of themselves. Such leaps are set-ups for failure, deep disappointment and, yes, more conflict. It seems that we just get more of what we don't know what to do with until we figure out what to do with it.

How Women "Do" Conflict

Some generalizations can be made about how sex roles influence our ways of dealing with conflict. Overall, women are taught to avoid conflict and get their way with indirect maneuvering, manipulation or by "being good." Persistence is not valued, getting along is. Women are taught that to be direct and to show anger is pushy, bitchy, unfeminine and suspect. Men, on the other hand, are taught to bully, to dominate, and to be forceful and commanding to get their way. Persistence is valued. Accommodation, compromise and "backing down" are seen as cowardly, unmanly and suspect.

Lesbians also experience sex-role conditioning but it plays out in different ways. It's generally true that the more butch a sister is the more she will have incorporated the male style of "doing conflict", with both it's positive directness and problematic one-up-manship. The more femme-identified will tend towards cajoling, nagging or "going around" but will also have a heightened ability to process and express difficult feelings. While we all have a combination of these attributes, sex role identification and upbringing will influence our predominant styles.

Expressed conflict in heterosexual relationships is minimized by adhering to assumed gender roles of behavior. When those roles are changed or broken, conflict increases. In modern lesbian relationships, there are far fewer prescribed roles and there is more room for confusion and conflict.

EXERCISE 50 — *What Gender Roles Were You Served?* ♀

1. Which gender roles concerning conflict have most influenced you?

2. What other sex role messages have you received about conflict?

Valuing Conflict

Conflict feels uncomfortable to most of us. Our discomfort is usually from fear that our needs will not be met or from previous experience with destructive conflict. But conflict isn't all bad, though that may be hard to remember when one's adrenaline skyrockets and defenses go up. Conflict has positive purposes and possibilities. It simply indicates differences. Some differences enhance a relationship, and some are blocks that need to be resolved.

Our relationship to conflict is shaped by past trauma we've experienced and by the presence or lack of healthy role models. Many women have experienced abusive conflict and therefore either avoid it in general, act it out abusively, or do both.

(Continued on page 138)

Exercise 51 — *Conflict Tolerance*   ♀/♀♀

This exercise will help you become conscious of your own responses to specific types of expressed conflict.

Read the following responses to conflict. Using the table on the next page, rate your reaction to each one on a scale ranging from 1 to 5, as described. Share your observations with your partner — it will help you understand each other better.

Not all of these expressions are desirable or constructive for everyone. Emotional and physical safety are necessary for conflict to be resolved constructively.

1 = "It doesn't bother me a bit."
2 = "It bothers me slightly."
3 = "It makes me quite uncomfortable, but I can deal with it."
4 = "I can barely stand it. I get knots in my stomach, feel fear or numbness."
5 = "I can't stand it. I must leave the room either physically or emotionally."

	1-5		1-5	...DURING A CONFLICT
When I		When she		disagree(s)
When I	.	When she		feel(s) irritated
When I		When she		have/has angry feelings
When I		When she		feel(s) rageful, furious
When I		When she		use(s) a loud voice during conflict
When I		When she		have/has conflict in the car or another small place
When I		When she		have/has conflict in front of others
When I		When she		cry(s) during conflict
When I		When she		give(s) the "silent treatment" or withdraw(s) emotionally
When I		When she		desire(s) to verbally attack (without doing it)
When I		When she		desire(s) to push or hit (without doing it)
When I		When she		leave(s) the room during a conflict

Some women experience all conflict as frightening or abusive. Others may have grown up in a family that didn't allow negative feelings to be expressed. When confronted with conflict in their adult lives, they believe it to be abnormal or wrong, or immediately feel overwhelmed or at a loss.

Valuing constructive conflict is an integral part of healthy relationships. It helps couples maintain individuality. Our expressions and topics of conflict reflect our prior life experiences. Disagreements bring to the fore what we want, expect and assume, and what we fear. A relationship without any conflict often occurs when partners are not being honest with themselves or each other; they may have abandoned themselves in some way, gone 'underground' or kept emotionally distant.

The Need for Secure Connection

So much of the pain and fear that comes up during conflict is due to feelings of disconnection from our loved one. We come into this world with the fundamental need to have a secure connection with a primary and significant other. No matter how old we get we still feel lonely and anxious without it. A secure connection allows us safe haven when we are vulnerable and a firm base from which to venture out into the world. Humans are social beings, so we seek out these connections in partnerships, in community and extended family. This need is part of our neurobiology. Inter-dependence increases our species chance of survival. It is this fundamental need that we seek to fill in becoming emotionally intimate with another person.

Conflict often feels like a threat to this security — and sometimes it is. It hurts when we feel our beloved mis-perceives us, judges us or says that we don't measure up — and if we feel our connection with them is threatened, we can end up feeling not only hurt (or defensive), but terrified. A relationship that can resolve conflicts without threatening that connection builds a feeling of security and an ability to be intimate. All problems become more manageable when connections do not feel threatened. Thus, the more we can learn about our patterns of conflict the more we can change our perceptions and behaviors to make conflict less threatening and hurtful.

Confronting Assumptions

We develop many assumptions and beliefs about conflict based on our cultural and familial experiences. These can keep us from changing our behavior.

EXERCISE 52 — What Does It Mean To Me?   ♀/♀♀

Below are two lists.

Conflict means: _____	1. Someone gets hurt (physically or emotionally)
	2. Danger
Compromise means: _____	3. Loss
	4. Being attacked, or attacking
Louder voices mean: _____	5. Abandonment
	6. Rejection
Silence means: _____	7. Losing
	8. Winning
Winning means: _____	9. Being right
	10. Being wrong
Differences mean: _____	11. Humiliation or Shame
	12. Being "weak"
Fighting means: _____	

1. Choose the meanings (or mis-assumptions) that the words in the left-hand column have for you by matching them with items in the right-hand column. Write the numbers indicating the meaning of it to it's right.

2. Read your responses over and think about how these beliefs influence your perceptions and behaviors during conflict or potential conflict.

3. Share these ideas with your partner if you wish.

While these beliefs are born of real, yet subjective, experiences, they are not necessarily helpful to us in relationships. Sometimes conflict does lead to emotional or physical casualties, and differences can mean there will be loss or rejection; they are not, however, absolute truths. Beliefs and behavior can be changed in order to make conflict resolution constructive and rewarding.

The first step toward making changes is becoming conscious of ones beliefs and the effects of those beliefs. The next step is to let go of or rebuild the beliefs with destructive consequences. To change beliefs that hinder you start by understanding how your current situation differs from the ones in which the beliefs were formed. Remind yourself of this often and tell yourself a more calming or useful idea each time conflict comes up.

Win/Lose or Win/Win?

The concept of winning and losing plays an important role in our attitudes toward conflict. Valuing conflict does not mean valuing "being right." The idea that "winning" an argument makes the winner correct is not logically valid. But winning and "being right" have a powerful place in the dominant culture. We are trained to think critically by invalidating others' points of view, by tearing apart the logic of their statements. This creates a situation where one can be either right or wrong with no room for different paradigms or perceptions.

EXERCISE 53 — Assumptions About Being Right or Wrong ?

1. What beliefs do I have about being right or wrong? Where did I get those ideas?

2. In what ways would I like to change these beliefs? How would that help me?

3. What can I tell myself to begin this change? What can I do differently?

Willingness to Work Things Out

Avoiding or terminating conflict is not the same as resolving conflict. Resolution is a process that brings long-term satisfaction, while excessive avoidance or early termination bring only short-term comfort. The key to this process is built upon developing emotional skills, having the willingness to work things out and having the abilities and values listed below.

- ▾ sharing and revealing oneself
- ▾ understanding another perspective
- ▾ appreciating or showing appreciation
- ▾ having patience for letting everyone have a say
- ▾ valuing diversity (respecting another's ideas while holding onto your own)
- ▾ contributing, giving ideas
- ▾ checking for understanding
- ▾ checking for agreement or lack of agreement
- ▾ being open to influence
- ▾ being able to bring up problems in a non-blaming manner
- ▾ willingness to make a repair if things go awry (eg. apologize, recognize the problem, try again)

This is a short list, but it is not one to read quickly. Most would agree that these items require some emotional maturity.

Pause & Reflect

EXERCISE 54 — Conflict Skills and Values   ♀/♀♀

Talk with your partner about each of the above listed abilities and values. Take turns answering these questions:

1. Which of these abilities/values have I mastered?

2. Which do I need to work on?

3. Why are these particularly difficult for me?

Pause & Reflect

4. What am I afraid will happen if I...
   ▾ reveal myself?
   ▾ appreciate you?
   ▾ see your perspective?
   ▾ let everyone have a say?
   ▾ value your differences?
   ▾ contribute my ideas?
   ▾ check for understanding?
   ▾ check for consensus or lack of consensus?
   ▾ am open to influence?
   ▾ bring up problems in a non-blaming manner?
   ▾ re-approach to make a repair if things go awry?

5. What would help me improve in these areas?

Negotiation

Negotiation is a tried and true way of resolving conflicts in a constructive manner. Negotiation can take any of these forms:

- Sharing: We can both do it. (For those who like control, this is hard.)

- Taking turns: We can do it your way this time and my way the next time. (Impatience makes this one difficult.)

- Compromising: Give up some and get some. (An all or nothing attitude doesn't work.)

- Using chance: Flip a coin or toss the dice. (Gamblers like this until they lose.)

- Seeking outside help: Let's ask someone else. (Difficult if you believe conflicts are to be hidden from outsiders.)

- Postponing: Later, when we cool down, we can deal with this. (Takes self-control.)

- Agreeing to disagree...with respect. (Differentiation is needed for this.)

- Using humor: Express it humorously, but not at the expense of another person. (Levity helps.)

EXERCISE 55 — *20/20 Hindsight*   ♀/♀♀

Answer the first five questions individually and numbers 6 and 7 with your partner.

1. Which items from the list on the previous page were used for negotiation in my family of origin?

2. Which ones have I practiced in my adult life?

3. Which ones am I best at?

4. Which am I worst at?

5. What makes the ones I am not good at particularly difficult for me?

6. With your partner, choose something from the list that you would like to do more often.

7. Think of a recent conflict you've had and talk about how you might have resolved things differently. Make up a scenario of how it might have gone.

Getting Your Needs Met

As humans we all have needs and desires. Affirming and acting on these contributes to relationship health. There is nothing wrong with attempting to get our needs and desires met and fulfilled as long as our means are not destructive and do not infringe on others' rights. It is when our needs or desires are in conflict with our partner's needs or desires that the work begins.

EXERCISE 56 — Getting Your Needs Met

This nine-step process will help you in your attempts to get your needs met and maintain the integrity of the relationship. It includes the elements of self-reflection, describing the problem and the feelings, making a request, using communication skills, negotiating and setting up a trial period.

1. **Get Clear with Yourself:** Get clear on what's going on inside yourself. Ask yourself questions about your feelings, your defenses, the "problem," your wants, etc. Writing, talking with a friend, thinking or meditating are all good ways to get clear.

2. **Initiate a Meeting:** Request a meeting to discuss/resolve the conflict or issue. Set a time limit to the discussion.

3. **State the Problem:** Stick to the facts, and don't use blaming. Don't express your feelings yet; check your tone and voice level.

4. **State Your Feelings:** Use "I" statements. Avoid blaming in your word selection, tone of voice and body language. Acknowledge any other unrelated factors/history that might contribute to your emotional reactions.

5. **Make a Specific Request:** Make your request simple and clear. Be as specific as possible. What change or behavior do you desire? (For example, you'd like more affection. Give examples of how that can be demonstrated.) If you have no specific ideas of how to solve the problem, go directly to step 6 and use active listening to explore feelings. Then, brainstorm solutions together, sharing all of the possibilities; even the crazy ones. Pick one to try, and proceed to step 8.

6. **Use Active Listening with Each Other:** Listen to reactions. Make sure you both understand the problem by restating what you thought you heard.

7. **Respond and Negotiate:** Make counter-proposals, set clear limits, don't agree to anything you're not genuinely willing to try (don't agree just to make peace).

8. **Set a Trial Period:** Set a period to try this out. Include check-in times to evaluate how it's going. Set a time for renegotiating or renewing the agreement.

9. **Clarify the Agreement:** It is very important to have the specifics of your agreement clear with the other person. Restate the agreement even if it seems silly to do so. In most cases, it's best to write it down.

Fighting

Fighting is a form of conflict resolution. It is an important expression of emotions, sometimes leading to a helpful solution of the problem but more often leading to hurt and misunderstanding. Without conscious parameters, fighting can be destructive, escalating reactions rather than encouraging considered responses to the situation.

Everyone defines fighting a little bit differently. The definition can range from blatant emotional, verbal or physical abuse on one end of the spectrum to mild disagreements or differences of opinion on the other. Without attempting to create an absolute definition, we present some parameters that will help your fighting become more productive, more tolerable, and perhaps, at times, even energizing.

Most of us know more about unfair fighting than we do about fair fighting. Our cultural conditioning toward competition and the goal of being "right" in adversarial situations does not serve us in intimate relationships. This conditioning seriously interferes with our creating the collaborative and loving partnerships we seek.

Avoidance of conflict also creates a fertile environment for unfair fighting as difficult feelings, unmet needs and unexplored differences go underground. In spite of our best efforts at suppression, these concerns leak out, and always with corrosive effect. Too often indirect anger, resentment and hurt become the invisible pilots of our communication.

There are many types of unfair fighting, and while so engaged we may not have any idea of what we are doing. You can use this list to start identifying ways that you contribute to messy and hurtful exchanges.

Unfair Fighting Methods

This list has been adapted and expanded from a pioneering, self-published pamphlet named *The Lesbian Relationship Handbook* by P.J. Kinheart Athey and M.J. Kinheart Osterman (Kinheart POSH, 1984).

Gunnysacking

Stuffing all of your annoyance and irritation into a "gunnysack" until your sack is full, and then exploding with all of the stored-up anger over one (often minor) issue.

Kitchen Sink

Dragging all of the problem issues into one fight and making clarity (or resolution) impossible.

Win-Lose

Approaching a fight assuming that only one person can win — and it's going to be me!

Below The Belt

Hitting your partner's emotional soft spots (vulnerabilities), reminding them of former "failures" or using information given to you in a moment of extreme vulnerability against them.

Withdrawal

This takes several forms, including leaving emotionally, giving "the silent treatment," walking out physically, and ignoring your partner's attempts to engage you. It is not the same thing as taking a "time-out" from the fight. (Note: Walking out is acceptable if there is any threat of violence. It is recommended as a mutually agreed-upon method to stop escalation before violence occurs.)

Indirect

Includes fighting about things other than the real issue, using emotions to manipulate, using sarcasm and baiting, coercing, employing acts of sabotage such as "forgetting" plans, not following through on promises.

Pushing Emotional Boundaries

Insisting that an issue continue to be dealt with immediately, even when one or both of you are emotionally exhausted, overwhelmed or too confused to go on. Insisting on continuing a fight when it is nonproductive.

Pushing Physical Boundaries

Staying so close to your partner when anger is present that you or they feel threatened by close proximity. (This is particularly important when dealing with survivors of any abuse.)

Condescending/Placating

Any form of discounting or minimizing the other's feelings or experience. This comes out in statements such as: "you're just upset because you're getting your period," "you just had a bad day at work, honey," "whatever you want, dear," "get over it," etc.

Killing Them With Kindness

This is a variation of placating that is quite toxic. This is acting *so* rational, *so* aloof and *so* in control that it leaves the other person feeling crazy for having feelings.

Self-Deprecating

This is responding to another's criticism or concerns by excessively putting oneself down, leaving no room for constructive dialogue or negotiation.

Name-Calling

Calling someone nasty names, put-downs and general devaluation of the other person is counter-productive and emotionally abusive.

Physical Contact

Physical contact during a fight is rarely appropriate. Slapping, pushing, shoving, punching and hitting of any kind are all physically abusive behaviors. Throwing or breaking objects in close proximity to another is an indirect threat of physical violence and is also abusive. Offering physical affection or comfort to an angry person is an option, but rejection of this offer must be respected.

Passive-Aggressive

Acquiescence with attitude. Appearing accommodating or neutral while there is underlying resistance and this anger leaks out in forms such as veiled insults; lack of follow-through on commitments; critical comments that are seemingly unrelated to the issue at hand.

Under The Influence

Attempting to resolve conflict while under the influence of chemical substances (including alcohol, marijuana, many prescription and non-prescription drugs) is pretty much a waste of time since thinking is impaired and feelings are often magnified out of proportion. Impulse control is also compromised, so escalation of fights and usually uncharacteristic behaviors are common.

EXERCISE 57 — Working It Out

1. Identify which of the above unfair fighting methods were used in your family of origin.

2. Which ones do you still use?

Pause & Reflect

3. Pick one of the offending habits to focus on in the upcoming weeks. Invent three ways to concretely work on changing this habit. (For example, notice that you're doing it, take a time-out whenever the behavior starts, use deep breathing, say "stop" to yourself or out loud, visualize the situation without the use of unfair fighting, go get a drink of water.)

All unfair fighting methods are a result of defensive thinking and behavior. When we feel threatened, misunderstood, attacked or blamed we resort to defensive survival patterns. When we realize that these patterns are learned, we can more easily break the cycle of shame, fear and then anger and blame which perpetuate these defensive reactions. We must be able to admit to the problem before we can solve it.

When Does Conflict Become Abusive?

The previous pages say a lot about how *not* to fight. These "unfair" methods range from annoying to destructive. There is however a category of behavior that is necessary to mention — emotional and verbal abuse.

Emotional/Verbal Abuse Is One or More of These:

- harmful to self-esteem
- harmful to personal resources, i.e. friends, money, possessions, family connections
- manipulative with a threat to physical or emotional well being
- harassment (repetitive confrontation with an attempt to intimidate)

Emotional abuse is sometimes even harder than other abuse to define and recognize. Almost everyone does it at some time or other and many couples develop a habit of hurling insults at each other. It's often hard to determine who did what to whom first, especially if the injury is delivered in a subtle way. If you find that you are experiencing any of these we suggest you seek professional help. First individual counseling to get safe and sort it out, and then, possibly, couples counseling. This list is excerpted from *Getting Free: You Can End Abuse and Take Back Your Life* by Ginny McCarthy (Seal Press, WA. 1990).

How many of these things has your partner done to you?

- ignored your feelings
- ridiculed or insulted you on a regular basis (including sarcasm)
- ridiculed or insulted your most valued beliefs, your religion, race, heritage or class
- withheld approval, appreciation or affection as punishment
- continually criticized you, called you names, shouted at you
- insulted or driven away your friends or family
- humiliated you in private or public
- refused to socialize with you
- kept you from working, controlled your money, made all decisions
- refused to work or share money
- took car keys or money away

▼ regularly threatened to leave or told you to leave

▼ threatened to hurt you or your family

▼ punished or deprived the children when angry at you

▼ threatened to kidnap the children if you left

▼ abused pets to hurt you

▼ told you about affairs (assuming you did not want to know)

▼ harassed you about affairs she imagined you were having

▼ manipulated you with lies and contradictions

If you did some of these things to your partner as well, the picture might be confusing. But the first thing to recognize is whether you were abused. Once you see that, you can evaluate the consequences. If you're still in the relationship or have only recently left it, you might not be able to tell yet what the long-range damage is, but answering the following questions may give you some ideas about it.

Did you often doubt your judgment or wonder if you were "crazy"? Were you often afraid of your partner and did you express your opinion less and less freely? Did you develop fears of other people and tend to see others less often? Did you spend a lot of time watching for her bad, and not so bad, moods before bringing up a subject? Did you ask permission to spend money, take classes or socialize with friends, and have fears of doing the wrong thing or getting in trouble? Did you lose confidence in your abilities, become increasingly depressed and feel trapped and powerless?

If you answered "Yes" to many of these question it's probable you have changed as a result of being abused. If you feel you deserved to be abused because you also abused your partner, consider that your actions don't negate the problem. Rather, they indicate you have two problems, your abuse and hers. If you make a commitment to respect and protect yourself, you may find yourself being less abusive, as well.

How to Fight Fair

Feelings of being threatened, attacked or blamed usually come with perceptions of powerlessness and/or ineffectiveness. The following methods and skills are most effective when both parties use them. (If only one person uses the following methods and practices the following skills, there will still be significant benefits.) Whoever uses these skills will find that ease and proficiency increase with practice. Although these methods can be challenging, they are guaranteed to save you emotional wear and tear.

Fair Fighting Methods

Win-Win

Assume a win-win possibility, a situation in which you can come to a mutually satisfactory resolution with no losers. Even if you don't end up agreeing to anything it can be mutually satisfying to each be heard and understood.

Choose Your Time

Pick a time and place (private) when you both are ready to deal with the conflict.

Clarify

Name the issue as clearly as you can before you begin.

Own Up

Claim your own feelings with opening phrases such as "I feel..." or "When you...".

Be Direct

Use lots of "I" statements that express your needs and wants.

I feel...

I want...

I need...

I can't tolerate...

I would appreciate...

I prefer...

Check Your Assumptions

Be sure, by restatement or repetition of the other's statements, that you really hear and understand her position (this does not mean you must agree).

Time Outs

Call a "time-out" or cooling-off period if the fight becomes manipulative or destructive, if there is no real listening, or if you become overwhelmed. "Time-outs" are to be previously agreed on as a safe method for taking breaks, not for avoiding the issue. A time-out can be called by either person, but there must be a return time designated to get back to the issue at hand. (This could be as short as five minutes or as long as a couple of days.)

Respect Boundaries

Honor physical boundaries and needs for time-outs. Accept your partner's comfort and safety limitations (if she tells you you're standing too close, back up; if she needs a time-out, don't argue).

Slow Down, Don't Interrupt, Use A Talking Stick

This is a good method for slowing down the process, being heard and avoiding interrupting each other. The person holding the baton (stick, rock, shell or any designated object) says three to five sentences while the other listens. The baton is then passed and the other person says three to five sentences. This continues until nothing is left to be said. An alternative method is to let the baton be held for as long as each person desires, until each runs out of things to say, and then the stick is passed.

Cry, Yell (If Tolerated)

Crying or loud voices can be fine during a fight if both partners tolerate it well. In some cultures these things are an expected part of a fight and don't necessarily hinder its progress or productivity. A person can be loud and not say abusive things; a person can cry and talk at the same time. The rule of thumb here is to modify the behavior or take a time-out if volume or crying becomes threatening to either person or somehow impedes resolution.

We often only stop to consider fair fighting methods when unfair fighting has taken a serious toll. Pain provides one of the strongest incentives to try new methods. However, when a couple is mired in unfair fighting and feelings are hurt, it can be one of the hardest times to find the courage and presence to try new ways of relating. The following exercises are designed to familiarize you with fair fighting and to make emergency applications easier.

EXERCISE 58 — Experimenting With Fair Fighting   ♀

1. Select two or three of the items from the fair fighting list on the previous page that you are willing to try. Write them here.

2. Imagine a conflicted interaction you might find yourself in over the next week or so. Where would your key fair fighting items be applicable?

3. Imagine how you would introduce them into the situation. How would it feel?

Pause & Reflect

4. How can you remind yourself of the items you've chosen to focus on? Some methods are writing notes to yourself and putting them in places you'll see; assigning symbols or animals to the various methods for easy memory devices; talking about your plans to use them with your partner or other friendly cohorts. List other ways that may be useful to you.

5. Notice the outcomes as you experiment with these methods. And give yourself credit for trying some new ways.

EXERCISE 59 — Using Fair Fighting in a Crunch ♀/♀♀

Do this part individually:

1. Think back to the last time you heard yourself reacting in those now-familiar, nasty, defensive patterns with your partner.   *Pause & Reflect*

2. Select one of the fair fighting methods you feel would have been helpful. Imagine using it.

3. Imagine a more positive outcome. (Such positive outcomes are not guaranteed in real life, but they are more probable if you try.)

Do this part with your partner, as needed:

1. The next time you find yourself or your partner taking a defensive position, ask to take a short break — even 30 seconds can make a big difference.

2. Select and discuss one of the fair fighting methods you believe may be helpful. If your partner is resistant to the idea, select one of the methods you can apply by yourself.

3. Notice your own experience. What was easy and what was difficult about using fair fighting? How did you feel after trying it? Ask your partner what her experience was. Be kind to yourselves by letting go of expectations of perfection. Everything has a beginning.

4. Congratulate yourself (or yourselves) for venturing into new territory and setting the stage for fewer frayed nerves and a more satisfying resolution.

Take Heart

We are all unique in our preferences and needs, we all have vulnerabilities and defenses, we all have our limitations. Given that, sooner or later we come into conflict with those nearest and dearest to us. Courageously experimenting and learning productive ways of addressing our differences enable us to value and recognize conflict's positive purposes.

Productive conflict resolution requires good communication and emotional skill that allow us to lower our defenses, to express our needs, show appreciation and let each have a say. These tools value diversity and enable us to check for mutual understanding and consensus. Negotiation skills and selecting a supportive time and environment are also important.

Recognizing and avoiding unfair fighting are the first steps to successfully utilizing fair fighting approaches. But learning takes time and practice. Changing our patterns of conflict is a learning process that we experience in fits and starts. We find ourselves smoothly articulating our needs and appreciation during one interaction only to shut down or froth at the mouth in the next. Allow yourself and the one you find lovable yet frustrating plenty of understanding and congratulations for your well-intended attempts. Intimate relationships are considered the graduate school of being human and, by nature, challenge our abilities.

What's It Worth?

Relationships, primary and otherwise, can serve as higher education, an intensive course in self-awareness and personal growth. It is in relationship that we have one of the most accessible ways to develop spiritual, emotional and mental acuity. Most of us wish to enter this school of learning at some time in our lives.

Our need for connection with others is hard-wired into the brain to enhance our chances for health and survival. Yet relationships are far more than survival strategies.

We are vastly enriched by interdependence and communion with one another. Indeed, primary relationships can be healing experiences, therapeutically healing previously hurtful relationships with family and partners. To approach a primary romantic relationship as the answer to life's sorrows or as the completion of the self is, however, most often problematic. Find those aspects of living which bring you meaning and purpose, spirit and heart, in order to create an internal environment where relationships can flourish. The balance between too much involvement in any relationship and too much distance is determined by each couple as they struggle to define the meaning of their union and find their own level of comfort and healthy interdependence.

Self-esteem, a sense of self, and a desire for inter-relatedness are helpful qualities to bring to a relationship. If you fall short of these, take heart; a loving relationship can foster self-esteem, identity and desire to connect intimately. Conscious relating means being aware of yourself, your triggers and patterns, your areas of lack and areas of strength. It also means having the willingness to look again at another person with a fresh perspective (re-spect), with eyes free from judgment and full of compassion. It means making the effort to truly understand one another, rather than look for confirmation of the "understanding" one already has. This brings about growth and healing on the deepest levels.

While the need to value one's individuality and respect differences is important, a relationship will only work if both members also value their common good and place safe, loving connection as a priority. In the maturing of a relationship the focus on individual needs must be balanced with values of family, culture and community. Dependency is not a "dirty" word. Human beings are social creatures who need each other. A loving relationship is one in which you help each other to be your best, nurture each other's strengths, and soothe and sometimes protect each other's vulnerabilities. It is one you can depend on for companionship, respect, acceptance and help.

Each individual carries with her a complex interplay of her past learning, her self concept, her values, her present situation and culture. Therefore each time two people commit to relating it presents a situation with unique rewards and challenges. Though no two couples are the same there are commonalities of experience we can learn from each other. In this workbook I have attempted to share some of these common issues, problems and solutions for lesbian relating.

Whether you have read through from start to finish or used this book as an occasional reference I hope that your journey through it has been a beneficial one.

Using This Book In a Therapeutic Setting

- Peer Groups
- Professionally Facilitated Groups
- Guidelines for Choosing a Counselor and Being in Counseling

Peer Groups

Times

I suggest meeting once a week, for 8–9 weeks (minimum); meetings of 1½ – 2 hours work best. Your group can be a group of four (two couples) up to seven or eight women (I don't recommend any more for a non-facilitated group). Use the chapters in consecutive order. Schedule time regularly to evaluate the group as it proceeds.

Guidelines

Guidelines provide group safety by establishing norms of behavior and affirming principles of respect. Distribute these to each member before the group starts and discuss them on the first meeting.

This group is designed to provide:

- ▾ a forum for lesbians to share their own experiences of being in relationships and to hear that of other's
- ▾ information on relationship skills and specific issues pertinent to lesbian relationships
- ▾ a safe place to experiment with and practice relationship skills

The power and effectiveness of any group process is relative to the degree of open communication and honesty. Group members are encouraged to be open and honest with themselves and with other members. However, honesty requires safety and protection. Honesty without regard for others feelings can be abusive. The following guidelines help ensure group and member safety.

1. **Confidentiality:** You are free to share your own issues and experiences outside the group but are not free to divulge identifying or personal information regarding any other members (including your partner's).

2. **Freedom of Expression:** You are free to ask anything, and others have the right not to answer.

3. **Group Interaction:** You are encouraged to speak from your feelings and experiences. Listen to others as much as possible without judging; share feeling and responses you have to others' stories/ feelings, refrain from advice or criticism.

4. **Participation:** Personal experience is the most powerful and lasting means of growth. You can choose to share and participate as much or as little as you wish. While you can discuss your own responses and experiences outside group sessions, you are strongly encouraged to bring those same topics and feelings back to the group. The more involved you are as a group participant, the higher your chances of gaining from the experience of being in a group. Because it limits participation, it is preferable that couples don't make secret-keeping agreements between themselves.

5. **Right To Decline:** Each member always has the right to say "no" to any exercise or request. If you are feeling overwhelmed or out of control, you are encouraged to take a "time-out" by stating that you are unable or unwilling to continue communication at this time. This allows protection and honesty at the same time.

6. **Active Observation:** If you choose not to participate directly in an exercise you can be an "active observer." This means watching the group process and giving feedback later, and/or focusing on one other person in order to gain a sense of empathy for what they are experiencing.

7. **Unacceptable Behavior:** There will be no violence, no threat of violence and no deliberate cruelty or verbal abuse (including truth without regard for the other person) tolerated in group sessions.

8. **Alcohol/Drug Use:** Members are asked to abstain from alcohol and other mood-altering drugs/substances for the 12-hour period preceding each meeting.

9. **Personal Responsibility:** During open discussion time you are responsible for bringing up your own issues and concerns. Group members should speak only for themselves and their experience, trusting that their partner and other group members can express and identify their own feelings, thoughts and concerns. If

a member feels that her privacy is being compromised by her partner's sharing, that member is expected to do her best to speak up on her own behalf at that time.

10. **Commitment:** Each member and each couple is asked to make this group a priority and to make a commitment to the full number of designated weeks for the group.

11. **Fees:** If there are costs involved (such as room rental) fees should be paid in advance. Each person or couple is asked to purchase their own workbook (please do not photocopy workbooks—the author depends on your goodwill and hard cash).

12. **Absences:** Punctuality is very important as late arrivals disrupt the group activity and prevent all members from receiving the full benefit of each meeting. If you must miss a session, tell the group in advance or leave a message with one of the participants prior to the meeting.

13. **Termination:** If you and/or your partner must leave the group before your commitment ends, inform the members as soon as possible. Attendance for a minimum of one week after the announcement is expected for good-byes and closure.

Format

Identify a timekeeper for each meeting. (It's a good idea to rotate this task.) Begin promptly; don't wait for stragglers or the group will get started later and later each week. Similarly, end promptly so that people don't get too worn out or resentful of disregarded boundaries; if a topic is not finished, continue it at the next meeting.

You may want to designate someone each meeting to be the "facilitator." This can be rotated at each meeting so that no one takes on that role too exclusively. The person acting as facilitator helps deal with difficult feelings or acts as a mediator between parties and maintains the agreed upon format. If participants adhere to rules about giving each other feedback in respectful ways then the facilitator's job is not too arduous.

The structure outlined below has evolved as a successful one. You may wish to amend it depending on your needs and goals.

1. **Begin:** Start each session with a meditation or quiet reflection for five to ten minutes.

2. **Check-in:** Go around the group, each person saying briefly how they are at this time and offering any pertinent information about the couples' activities from the preceding week.

3. **Follow up:** Give time to get feedback or complete unfinished business from previous issues or group interactions.

4. **Topic:** Have someone introduce the topic for the meeting, based on the reading done at home. Summarize the main concepts.

5. **Discussion:** Discuss the topic, sharing personal experiences and ideas or opinions.

6. **Exercises:** Choose one or two exercises to do during group time.

7. **Sharing:** Come back together to share your experiences.

8. **Homework:** Decide on the reading and exercises to do for homework.

9. **Closure:** End each session with a closure/check-out time. This is a time for each person to say how the meeting affected them, how they are doing, or to evaluate the group.

Professionally Facilitated Groups

These additions/changes to the guidelines listed above are recommended if you use this book in a professionally facilitated group.

Fees: The fee for each group session is $__ per person. (I recommend a sliding fee scale based on the financial resources of the participant). Fees should be paid in advance unless otherwise arranged with the facilitator. Fees cover the cost of room rental and the time of the professional facilitator. Each person or couple is expected to provide her own workbook.

Absences: If you must miss a session you are asked to tell the group in advance or leave a message with the facilitator(s) prior to the group meeting. Absences are not deductible from the group fees. Punctuality is very important, as late arrivals disrupt the group activity and prevent all members from receiving the full benefit of each session.

Guidelines for Choosing a Counselor and Being in Counseling[1]

Deciding to go into therapy and finding a counselor can be challenging. Give yourself time to think and feel about whom you are interviewing. You may want to write in a journal, or talk to friends about the process.

Interview several professionals and focus on finding someone you feel comfortable with. If you can, talk with three different people.

Questions To Ask

These questions do not have *right* answers. By asking these questions you can get a preliminary sense of their work and if you might feel comfortable working with them.

1. What type of therapy/counseling do you practice? What are your specialties?

2. What training have you had? What are your credentials?[2]

3. How can you help me with my issues? Have you worked with other people with similar issues?

4. Have you worked with lesbians or lesbian couples before? How often?

5. What do you think is different between working with lesbians and working with heterosexual women?

6. How will you and I know when it's time to end counseling?

7. What can I do if I don't like the counseling?

8. What is the cost, how are increases handled, and what options do I have if the fee is too high for me?

After talking with each person, ask yourself:

1. Did I feel the counselor listened to what I said I needed?

2. Can this person help me with what I want? (Be careful if someone tries to convince you that you need what she or he is offering and not what you think you need.)

3. How comfortable did I feel talking with this person?

4. If I ever had a concern about therapy could I imagine voicing it to this person?

If you can, actually meet with the person in his or her office. Then you can ask yourself: "how did the space feel to me?"

During therapy it is important to keep checking with yourself and your counselor to make sure it is working for you. Remember that while therapy is designed to promote change and to help people feel better, it is common for the experience to be challenging or even painful at times. Some questions to ask yourself:

1. Are you and your needs the focus of the time or does the counselor focus more on him/herself?

2. Are you the "expert" on your own body/feelings/thoughts, or does the counselor act as if she or he knows more about you than you do? The counselor should certainly have suggestions and be able to offer help, but the focus should be on your experience, not on what the counselor thinks about you. (Particularly if you don't feel entirely comfortable with their ideas about you.)

3. Counseling should not be a mystery. Is the therapist willing to talk about therapy in a way that makes it understandable to you?

4. Can you say no if she or he makes a suggestion you are uncomfortable with? If you are not able to say no, can you in any way (including writing) let the counselor know of your discomfort or of your difficulty saying no?

5. Have you ever felt the counselor has been inappropriate sexually; with suggestions, touch or questions?[3]

6. Do you feel free to end therapy when you want to, or to take a break for a while?

7. Are there goals for counseling that you feel you are both working toward?

---

1 Adapted from: *Guidelines for Choosing a Therapist and Being in Therapy*, Jan Ögren, MFT, SCWAR, 1994.

2 Licensed Therapists, Registered Interns and people with State Regulated Certificates must adhere to certain guidelines, and their clients have specific recourse to their regulating boards if they have a complaint about the counseling. For example; in California, Marriage and Family Therapists must follow a set of ethical and legal guidelines in the areas of maintaining confidentiality, clarifying fees in advance, avoiding harmful dual relationships, having no sexual contact, referring for issues beyond one's expertise and advertising accurately. **All** professionals should follow these guidelines no matter what credentials they have. Unlicensed or non-credentialed professionals do not have to adhere to any standard guidelines and it may be harder to take action if a client feels harmed by the experience. (There is always the possibility of civil or criminal suit, though that can be difficult to go through.) Unfortunately licensing/credentialing is not a guarantee of quality or ethical behavior, and you must use your best judgment, as well as possible second opinions, if you begin to suspect that something is not right in the work your counselor is doing with you. There are also unlicensed counseling professionals who are well trained, ethical and can be excellent. If you want to choose one of these counselors be sure to get detailed information about their training and work, and if possible, their local reputation.

3 In most states in the U.S. it is illegal for a licensed psychotherapist to have any sexual contact with a client. Whether illegal or not, it is unethical for any therapist (other than a sex therapist) to have any sexual contact with a client.

Help With Personal Skills

- Developing the Skill, Art and Benefits of Self-Management
- Insightful Speaking, Focused Listening
- Hypervigilance and Avoidance

Developing the Skill, Art and Benefits of Self-Management

The following material (pages 177–180) was developed by Peter M. Krohn, MFT, founder and director of *The Couples Center Educational Institute*, Sebastopol, CA.

People usually wait to figure out how to resolve conflicts in the heat and stress of the moment in which it's occurring. However, at that time your body is often going through a physiological arousal (no, not that kind). If your pulse is 10%, or more, above your normal baseline, your ability to respond is compromised (John M. Gottman, PhD). As your pulse increases, your ability to listen, think and understand has become seriously impaired (your body reacts in a fight, flight or freeze pattern). When this occurs, the most important priority is getting oneself calmed down. This needs to take precedence over anything else.

The goal of Self-Management is to avoid becoming emotionally reactive. People can become reactive in different ways; engaging in instantly escalating fights, or storming-off flights, passive aggressive acting-out, resentfully complying, issuing threats and ultimatums etc.

Self-Management means developing the skills: to tolerate pain and anxiety; to contain your negative reactions; to see your partner more objectively; and maintain a less defensive posture. These skills allow for the possibility of thinking clearly and productively, and responding compassionately.

Stumbling Blocks to Functioning at Your Best

- ▼ You are perceiving the situation in a way that has re-stimulated an old wound, hurt, etc. This may intensify your reaction to the current situation and explain why it feels disproportionately upsetting.

- ▼ The expectation that your partner validates, reflects and approves of you by agreeing or adopting your point of view. (This is actually an inability to see and/or treat your partner as a separate person, with their different feelings, thoughts, beliefs and values.)

- ▼ Taking things very personally. Believing that when your partner expresses complaints about you that it's *all about you*. (Rather than hearing it as an indication of how upset they're feeling in this moment.)

- ▼ Believing that the more you hear about your partner's upset feelings — the worse it will be. That you have to protect yourself by stopping your partner from building up a case against you, 'nipping it in the bud.'

- ▼ Difficulty putting yourself in your partner's shoes. It's really possible to do this and still hold onto your point of view — as you become successful you will enhance intimacy.

Self-Soothing Under Interpersonal Stress

Think of a typical, recurring stressful interaction between you and your partner. Focus on your feelings, thoughts and behavior — *then check any items from the list below that apply.*

Under stress, it's *mostly* true that I:

- ❑ think negative thoughts, blame, criticize or condemn my partner

- ❑ think negative thoughts, blame, criticize or condemn myself

- ❑ feel angry and express it instantly without thinking…blurt it out… have a nasty fight

- ❑ feel threatened, overwhelmed and leave the scene as quickly as possible

- ❑ say things that are unfair and inappropriate that I later wish I hadn't

- ❑ do things that I later regret or feel ashamed of

- ❑ re-enact a behavior that seems like a scene from my family when I was growing up

- ❑ get depressed, feel hopeless and stuck and do nothing
- ❑ resentfully comply to keep the peace
- ❑ go silent and withdraw
- ❑ become sarcastic and biting, then try to laugh it off
- ❑ try to forget it...keep smiling
- ❑ go numb, hold it in, hope to avoid any conflict
- ❑ distract myself
- ❑ talk to my friends instead of my partner
- ❑ tell myself "She could never handle my real feelings."
- ❑ make an attempt...then give up when I don't get understood
- ❑ get very upset...get flooded with everything that's ever been wrong
- ❑ do everything I can to avoid the feeling of having my nose rubbed in the dirt
- ❑ tell myself "She will never change...what's the use."
- ❑ don't feel much... nothing really bothers me
- ❑ change the subject
- ❑ get angry at someone or something else
- ❑ get busy...work harder...there's so much to do
- ❑ work on letting go and practicing non-attachment
- ❑ tell myself "I'll get even, eventually."
- ❑ think of the suffering of saints and others...life is dukha
- ❑ try not to let my partner see how bothered I really am
- ❑ drop hints, verbally or through my body language
- ❑ threaten to leave, or I console myself with thoughts of leaving
- ❑ use drugs and/or alcohol to "ease" the discomfort

Soothing "Self-Talk"

Other couples ideas of what helps them during stressful times.

"We are both in pain right now."

"I feel relief knowing I can take a short break anytime."

"It's hard for me to talk about some things. I remind myself that if I don't talk I will pull away and then I will feel alone. I want to be close so that helps me keep on talking."

"There are no bad guys."

"When it gets tough, I pretend I'm watching two other people talking to each other."

"I'm not responsible for what my partner is feeling. It's not *all* my fault."

"This too shall pass."

"What my partner feels right now, is not the whole picture, nor is it *all* of how she feels."

"I take a deep breath and think 'I'm O.K., I'm not a bad person. I don't have to be perfect."

"The important thing is to remember that underneath it all we both really want to feel safe and loved."

"I'm feeling reactive now, but I don't have to act it out. I can choose to stay calm."

What would be the most useful thing *for you to tell yourself,* that would help you stay more calm and centered if the situation were to happen again?

Insightful Speaking, Focused Listening

These are some of the common dilemmas faced by the Speaker.

Speaker's Dilemmas:

- blaming vs. complaining
- seeing yourself as the victim vs. seeing yourself as an active participant
- focusing on your partner as the problem vs. focusing on yourself as having a problem with your partner's behavior
- difficulty knowing one's inner self and/or having difficulty articulating your experience
- demanding agreement
- not connecting the situation at hand with a deeper understanding of self or couples dynamics

These are some of the common dilemmas faced by the Listener.

Listener's Dilemmas:

- problem solving or "fixing" the other person vs. sitting with the problem and learning more about it
- starting to talk about yourself vs. staying curious about the other
- managing your reactions in a respectful way vs. acting out defensively
- taking a complaint as an attack vs. an expression of your partner's difficulty/ discomfort/issues
- difficulty managing feeling misunderstood or misjudged vs. tolerating disappointment
- feeling terrible about yourself vs. maintaining your self-esteem

Hyper-Vigilance and Avoidance

Hyper-vigilance and avoidance are two coping mechanisms learned early in childhood. The purpose of these coping styles is to reduce anxiety. We are likely to have some combination of the two, but generally we tend towards one style more than the other. Often we partner with our opposite, which can cause much difficulty. Understanding the motivations behind the behaviors can increase compassion and help with maintaining perspective and patience.

The Hyper-Vigilant mind-set is: "Ignoring problems produces anxiety."

Therefore facing, discussing and fixing problems/issues helps in having a sense of control over life, schedule, environment, etc., thus reducing anxiety.

The Hyper-Vigilant person usually:

- hates conflict, seeks to eliminate it by focusing on it
- has a high degree of sensitivity to others moods (sometimes hypersensitive)
- has ability to self reflect
- has a good memory
- goes towards problems, wants to discuss thoroughly
- wants to be heard and validated as right
- anxiety moves into worry and rumination
- can't shut off thoughts
- doesn't know how to "self-soothe," depends on other for relief
- over-analyses, doesn't know when to back off
- holds onto topic (or maybe a grudge) like a bulldog

The Avoidant mind-set is "Facing problems produces anxiety, and can be confusing and overwhelming."

Therefore distracting or focusing on something other than the problem is soothing and anxiety reducing.

The Avoidant person usually:

- hates conflict and seeks to eliminate it by shutting it out
- anxiety quickly changes to non-feeling or confusion

182

- frequently wants to be left alone
- easily gets foggy/confused
- forgets things
- ignores conflict/problems ("they'll go away")
- has some self-soothing skills, primarily distraction
- likes quick resolution of conflict, to find a way to solve or "fix" it, ("so it will never happen again")
- distracts easily
- changes the subject

Quotable Women, Who Are They?

Elizabeth Akers Allen (October 9, 1832 — August 7, 1911) was an American author, journalist and poet. She began to write at the age of fifteen, under the pen name Florence Percy, and in 1855 published under that name a volume of poems entitled *Forest Buds*. In 1851 she married Marshall S.M. Taylor, but they were divorced within a few years. In subsequent years she travelled through Europe, in Rome she became acquainted with the feminist Paulina Kellogg Wright Davis. While in Europe she served as a correspondent for *The Portland Transcript* and *The Boston Evening Gazette*. In 1866 a collection of her poems was published in Boston.

Susan B. Anthony (February 15, 1820 – March 13, 1906) was a prominent, independent and well-educated American civil rights leader who played a pivotal role in the 19th century women's rights movement (the first wave of feminism) to secure women's suffrage in the United States. She traveled the United States and Europe, and gave 75 – 100 speeches per year on women's rights for some 45 years. Susan B. Anthony died in Rochester, New York in her house at 17 Madison Street on March 13, 1906, and is buried at Mount Hope Cemetery.

Edna Saint Vincent Millay (February 22, 1892 – October 19, 1950) was an American lyrical poet and playwright and the first woman to receive the Pulitzer Prize for Poetry. She was also known for her unconventional, bohemian lifestyle and her many love affairs. She used the pseudonym Nancy Boyd for her prose work.

Anaïs Nin (February 21, 1903 – January 14, 1977) was a French-born author who became famous for her published journals, which span more than 60 years, beginning when she was 11 years old and ending shortly before her death. Born Angela Anaïs Juana Antolina Rosa Edelmira Nin y Culmell, she is also famous for her erotica, which not only proves sensual, but also acts as a study of sexuality in its perfection and flaws.

Clementine Paddleford (September 27, 1898 – November 13, 1967) was an American food writer active from the 1920s through the 1960s, writing for several publications, including *The New York Herald Tribune*, *The New York Sun*, *The New York Telegram*, *Farm and Fireside*, and *This Week* magazine. A Kansas native, she lived most of her life in New York City, where she introduced her readers to the global range of food to be found in that city. She was also a pilot, and flew a Piper Cub around the country to report on America's many regional cuisines. She was well ahead of her time, matched as a regional-food pioneer only by James Beard, and her seminal book, *How America Eats*, appeared late in 1960.

Eleanor Roosevelt (October 11, 1884 – November 7, 1962) was an American political leader who used her influence as an active First Lady from 1933 to 1945 to promote the New Deal policies of her husband, President Franklin D. Roosevelt, as well as taking a prominent role as an advocate for civil rights. After her husband's death in 1945, she continued to be an internationally prominent author and speaker for the New Deal coalition. She was a suffragist who worked to enhance the status of working women, although she opposed the Equal Rights Amendment because she believed it would adversely affect women. In the 1940s, she was one of the co-founders of Freedom House and supported the formation of the United Nations. Eleanor Roosevelt founded the UN Association of the United States in 1943 to advance support for the formation of the UN. She was a delegate to the UN General Assembly in 1945 and chaired the committee that drafted and approved the Universal Declaration of Human Rights. President Harry S. Truman called her the "First Lady of the World" in tribute to her human rights achievements. She was one of the most admired persons of the 20th century, according to Gallup's List of Widely Admired People.

Muriel Rukeyser (December 15, 1913 – February 12, 1980) was an American poet and political activist, best known for her poems about equality, feminism, social justice, and Judaism. Kenneth Rexroth said that she was the greatest poet of her "exact generation." One of her most powerful pieces was a group of poems entitled *The Book of the Dead* (1938), documenting the details of the Hawk's Nest incident, an industrial disaster in which hundreds of miners died of silicosis. Her poem "To be a Jew in the Twentieth Century" (1944), on the theme of Judaism as a gift, was adopted by the American Reform and Reconstructionist movements for their prayer books, something Rukeyser said "astonished" her, as she had remained distant from Judaism throughout her early life.

Marianne Williamson (July 8, 1952) is a spiritual activist, author, lecturer and founder of The Peace Alliance, a grass roots campaign supporting legislation currently before Congress to establish a United States Department of Peace. She is also the founder of Project Angel Food, a meals-on-wheels program that serves homebound people with AIDS in the Los Angeles area. She has published nine books, including four of *The New York Times* #1 bestsellers.

The Two Wolves Within

A Cherokee Legend

An old Grandfather said to his grandson, who came to him with anger at a friend who had done him an injustice:

"Let me tell you a story.

I too, at times, have felt a great hate for those that have taken so much, with no sorrow for what they do.

But hate wears you down, and does not hurt your enemy. It is like taking poison and wishing your enemy would die. I have struggled with these feelings many times." He continued, "It is as if there are two wolves inside me. One is good and does no harm. He lives in harmony with all around him, and does not take offense when no offense was intended. He will only fight when it is right to do so, and in the right way.

But the other wolf, ah! He is full of anger. The littlest thing will set him into a fit of temper. He fights everyone, all the time, for no reason. He cannot think because his anger and hate are so great. It is helpless anger, for his anger will change nothing.

Sometimes, it is hard to live with these two wolves inside me, for both of them try to dominate my spirit."

The boy looked intently into his Grandfather's eyes and asked, "Which one wins?"

The Grandfather smiled and quietly said, "The one I feed."

CPSIA information can be obtained at www.ICGtesting.com
Printed in the USA
BVOW04s0452240915

419387BV00012B/5/P